Busy Fingers, Growing Minds

Finger Plays, Verses and Activities for Whole Language Learning

Rhoda Redleaf

Redleaf Press
a division of Resources for Child Caring

DISCLAIMER

Every effort has been made to identify copyrighted materials. Any omission is unintentional and will be corrected in future printings upon proper notification.

Published by: Redleaf Press
                 a division of Resources for Child Caring
                 450 North Syndicate, Suite 5
                 St. Paul, Minnesota 55104

Distributed by: Gryphon House
                 PO Box 275
                 Mt. Rainier, Maryland 20712

Cover photos by Susan Richman
Illustrations by Ellen Krans

ISBN: 0-934140-79-0

Library of Congress Cataloging-in-Publication Data

Redleaf, Rhoda
    Busy Fingers, Growing Minds : Finger Plays, Verses, and Activities
for Whole Language Learning / Rhoda Redleaf.
        p.   cm.
    "Over 160 Original Finger Plays and Verses."
    ISBN 0-934140-79-0
    1. Finger Play.   2. Language experience approach in education.
I. Title.
GV1218.F5R43 1993
793.9—dc20
                                        93-39636
                                          CIP

Printed in the United States of America.

This book is dedicated to
Nathaniel, Benjamin, Brian and Jonathan
who inspired many of these verses.

And to the memory of Deb Fish
who inspired and prodded me into writing in the first place.

Table of Contents

*ACTIVITIES

Chapter Two: From Home to School or Child Care

*ACTIVITIES

Chapter Three: Things that Work in the World

*ACTIVITIES

Chapter Five: A Few of My Favorite Things

*ACTIVITIES

*ACTIVITIES

Chapter Six: Changes All Around Me

*ACTIVITIES

*ACTIVITIES

Foreword

I am delighted to have been invited to write the foreword to Busy Fingers, Growing Minds. This marvelously creative book provides teachers with a wealth of practical ideas and strategies which can be used with children to enhance their understanding of the world.

I have known Rhoda Redleaf for over fifteen years and believe that she is uniquely qualified to create this book. She has spent her professional life not simply teaching, but also learning with both children and adults. She is a gifted teacher who consistently looks for creative, interesting and meaningful experiences for assisting both children and adults construct knowledge. Adults will especially appreciate her suggestions for "Conversation Starters," "Tips on Writing with Children," and the chapter, *Things that Work in the World.*

Her approach is a carefully conceived sequence of operational ideas and suggestions designed to help children make sense of their very complex and confusing worlds. Her thorough knowledge of children's development, their interests, their fears and concerns, keeps children at the core of all the activities. Skills are not taught in isolation nor are they avoided. Skills are integrated into the literature being recommended, the poetry being created, the dramatic play scenarios being enacted and the other creative activities suggested by the author. High quality written, oral and 'writing' opportunities are combined with many hands-on activities to provide interconnected and enjoyable opportunities for the support of language acquisition and emerging literacy. Throughout the entire book, the author's love of language and storytelling, and her respect for young children's experiences combine to inspire a text which is useful, practical, creative and fun.

By working through the suggestions and recommendations offered by Rhoda Redleaf in *Busy Fingers, Growing Minds,* teachers can instill in young children a love of learning and support their understanding of the world.

Lynn Galle
Coordinator, Early Childhood
Teacher Education Programs
University of Minnesota

Acknowledgements

It is difficult to acknowledge all the many people who have contributed in some way to the ideas, activities and verses included in this book. While most of the poems in this book are original, there are some that have been adapted from familiar fingerplays that somehow become part of the repertoire of all early childhood teachers. My mother was a kindergarten teacher and so I learned these type of poems as a very young child. She also would make up verses for my own children and these, too, became a part of me.

In my 35 years of teaching I have always enjoyed playing with language and many of my colleagues know that I could come up with a poem, song adaptation or fingerplay for any workshop, conference, class or special occasion. In the last 15 years of my work as a trainer, I wrote a monthly letter to our members which included verses, fingerplays and activities on a particular topic. Many of these verses first appeared in those newsletters along with some from other sources or from that vast area which many regard as common domain. I have tried to credit all verses that I think may have come from others, even when I have adapted them in some way. Memories are not always perfect, especially at my stage of development and if I have inadvertently included a verse without proper acknowledgment, I apologize and will be happy to correct any such error. Most of the traditional fingerplays and verses included in this book came from resources made available by the Minnesota Department of Human Services and the Minneapolis and St. Paul Public Schools' curriculum departments long, long ago. Others have been shared in hundreds of workshops over many years.

I would also like to acknowledge and thank those most closely involved in the production of this book. There is not a more outstanding editor than Eileen Nelson, whose patient prodding truly made this book possible. She is a miracle of organization and her tremendous knowledge of child development and appropriate programming makes her a most helpful resource. The production team of Alicia Raffel and Mary Pat Merabella did wonders with reorganization, structure, layout and design of a very amorphous and chaotic text. Copy editor Rosemary Wallner did a remarkable job of transforming my overly complex sentences into highly readable ones which conveyed the same meaning. Ellen Krans' wonderful illustrations add the perfect touch of directness, clarity and fun.

Finally, thank you to my family for their support and encouragement and especially to my husband, Paul, who patiently carried all my boxes of materials and my word processor back and forth from Chicago to St. Paul over the past several years of this work in process. His humorous prodding and interjections, while not necessarily speeding up the writing process, certainly made it more fun.

Introduction

Teachers of young children have long known the power of poetry to capture children's interest and attention. Infants, toddlers, and preschoolers respond quickly to the repetitive sounds of songs and verses from Mother Goose to our present-day Father Gander and beyond. What parent, grandparent, teacher, or caregiver hasn't delighted in a baby's gleeful anticipation of "This little piggy went wee-wee-wee all the way home"? If the words are accompanied by action—touching the baby's fingers or toes one by one and gently moving two fingers up the baby's arm or leg on the last line—the baby's reaction is intensified.

From this earliest beginning, "This Little Piggy" and other poems and finger plays continue to play an informative and organizing role in young children's lives. While the baby responds to the sensory stimulation of touch and the sound of the language, older children learn about the meaning of words (staying home, going to market); sequencing (what comes first, what comes next); and the idea that each finger or toe stands for one pig.

This latter concept (which is referred to as one to one number correspondence) is fundamental in developing an understanding of numbers. Numerous finger plays and stories such as "The Three Bears" play an important role in introducing children to numbers. Teachers and caregivers can expand upon all of these concepts in the preschool setting as they use simple puppets, props, or flannelboard figures to illustrate the verse and the ideas or associations in it. In this process, the children learn not only that the individual words have meaning and stand for something, but that they tell a story—one they may have enjoyed earlier on a purely sensory level. Numerous repetitions of familiar verses, adapted and used in many ways, can enhance children's development of understanding and fluency in language.

Of course, children must also learn to express their own ideas and use language to tell about their experiences. As you create and write down stories, finger plays, or poems, encourage the children to do the same. By making up their own stories, which are also written down and read, children develop better language skills and prepare themselves to read. Throughout this book, I encourage you to use the verses to explain things in your children's lives. Use the follow-up activities to encourage discussion and to write about the children's own experiences.

The process of telling, talking about, writing, reading children's dictated descriptions, and retelling is sometimes referred to as a *whole language approach*. It is an interactive approach that emphasizes eliciting children's responses to their experiences in their own words. Their own words may also include their "writing" about these experiences. Children can "read" this writing, which may be a variety of letters, lines, or scrolls, to an adult who can transcribe them into a more readable form. This notion of writing to read is successful in developing children's interest in reading. In addition, dictating to others (including stories they make up) and acting out things they have made up, promotes reading readiness and greater fluency in language in children.

Just as Mary Poppins told us that a "spoonful of sugar helps the medicine go down," many teachers know that a snappy verse helps children pick up blocks, straighten the room, and move themselves from here to there. Even when teachers and caregivers use finger plays to help organize children's activities, they still offer the same language learning potential. "Clean Up Time" to the tune of "Jingle Bells" (found in Chapter Two) is a perfect illustration of how to get the room picked up and use language to describe action at a familiar and basic level.

In addition to these beneficial, educational, and practical purposes, finger plays and verses are fun. I hope that the verses in this book will prove to be fun for you and your children. I want them to provide you with encouragement to play with words yourself. Create your own fun with language activities; create songs and finger plays that continually help your children make sense of their world.

A Few Tips on Writing with Children

Many of the activities included in this book suggest writing stories, drawing charts, designing books, and making lists. In fact, if you follow-up most activities as suggested, you will be writing with the children every day. Following are hints to help your group's writing time become productive and fun.

- Keep it short. You can write many sentences in a five- to ten-minute session. If you need more time, plan for a second brief session later. Reread and review your writing activity as often as you want. Children like hearing what they have written.

- Keep it simple. Use short sentences written in large print on newsprint- sized paper. One sheet is enough for children to write and read at a time.

- Keep it personal. Always use the child's name in the stories you write (Tommy's cat has white paws; Sue likes to ride ponies). Also, set aside some time to write with individual children. On their artwork, write the descriptions that they tell you. Write a quick account of something that just happened.

- Keep it. At least for a while, keep the stories, charts, books, and lists. Group writing about several children should be kept for the group. Decide if your writing activity is going into a group book or if it should be copied onto a smaller sheet of paper and kept in a writing file. Personal writings can go home if the child wants to take them home.

- Keep it posted. Let parents see these group writing activities. They give parents information about some things that the group did that day, which can lead to discussions between the parent and child.

- Keep it for other uses. The group may decide to use some of the writing activities for other projects. The writing may become signs for a bulletin board, display, or section of the room. You can use some of the things written to create group books. Use the parts you need and discard the rest.

- Keep it consistent. Use a specific area to write and keep a large marker and paper supply ready. Set aside a regular time to write, perhaps at group time. An exception would be when you are writing about a trip or other specific event that occurred after your usual writing time.

Making Homemade Books

You can make books in all different sizes and shapes using a variety of materials. The simplest procedure is to use two, three, or four sheets of paper folded in half and stapled together along the folded edge; the book's size varies with the size of the paper. I refer to many of the books in the following chapters as "Big Books." For these, use large, easel-sized paper. That size has room for large print and child-made illustrations, but is not too unwieldy when reading to the group.

You can create a more standard-sized book using 12" x 18" paper. Make small individual books using 9" x 12" paper. For another book style, use single sheets in any size and punch holes along one edge; hold the pages together with small rings or ribbon (ribbon is easier than yarn or string because the pages turn more smoothly). In each case, adapt the size of the printing to the paper, leaving room for children to make their additions.

Make a Ziploc baggie book by stapling together two, three, or four resealable bags along the left edge with the Ziploc part at the top. Insert pages by opening the baggie and slipping them in. The 10 1/2" x 11" storage bags work perfectly for 8 1/2" x 11" sheets of paper. Write on both sides of the pages and rewrite this book simply by changing the pages. Vary the size of the book by varying the size of the bags used and, if necessary, cut paper to fit.

You can also make books in loose-leaf notebooks, ringed folders, or term paper plastic holders. The latter are the hardest to use with young children because the side clasping bars are hard to use and pages frequently fall out. Use scrapbooks or photograph albums to create long-lasting books and books that you will add to over a period of time.

Felt tip pens are the best materials to use in printing your finished product, although you can use pencils in the children's own writings or in your preliminary efforts. I prefer to use a medium point marker for all of my writing with groups because it is easy to read.

Use lined or unlined paper, depending on which type you are most comfortable with. Unlined paper is more flexible and allows you to vary the size of your printing to the amount of content. Children don't seem to be bothered by printing that travels slightly up or down. Decorate the covers and pages in any way the children like.

Throughout this book, I have offered many suggestions on how to gather material to create homemade books. You can write books directly from the children's dictation or, for many projects, collect information first and then copy it over into the book format. If you lack material, use the verses to create the books. Choose a verse and copy a few lines onto each page of your book. Let the children add their pictures or comments to create a book that the children can read and reread.

CHAPTER ONE: All About Me

Introduction

*P*eople are the favorite topic of people to paraphrase a wise poet. This holds true for children as well as adults. In the case of young children, however, this interest focuses on a child in particular, themselves. Some of the earliest thoughts children express are "Me," "I," "Mine," and "Me do it." This is healthy and appropriate, and it is consistent with the goal of early childhood education, which is to help children develop good and positive feelings about themselves.

Many books have been written about the importance of high self-esteem, but many fail to translate that goal into daily practice. To enhance self-esteem, we must help children feel important, "I am important—my name, my teeth, my body, how I grow, how I feel, what I'm learning, things I'm curious about—everything about me is important. Not only am I important, but I am also worthy of having the things I do and learn tell about me."

If we are to follow the advice of sages from Alexander Pope to William Shakespeare to "know thyself," we will start by helping the youngest children learn more about themselves and how they grow. We will take the time to explain their names and other people's names. We will help them learn and appreciate things that we, as adults, often overlook. The verses and activities in this section are designed to help in that process.

When I Was Little

Two Little Eyes (*Traditional*)

Two little eyes that open and close	(*point to eyes and open and close them*)
Two little ears and one little nose	(*point to each*)
Two little cheeks and one little chin	(*point to each*)
And one little mouth that makes a big grin	(*everyone smile*)

Baby's Eyes (*Author Unknown*)

Blue-eyed babies	
Brown-eyed, too	(*point to eyes*)
Pat-a-cake	(*clap hands*)
And peek-a-boo	(*cover eyes and play peek-a-boo*)

Where Are Baby's Eyes?
(*to the tune of "Where Is Thumbkin?"*)

Where are baby's eyes? Where are baby's eyes?
Here they are, here they are   (*touch gently, corner of each eye*)
Where is baby's nose? Where is baby's nose?
Here it is, here it is   (*tap gently on nose*)

Where are baby's ears? Where are baby's ears?
Here they are, here they are   (*wiggle each ear lobe*)
Where is baby's mouth? Where is baby's mouth?
Here it is, here it is   (*touch each side of mouth*)

Add verses about other body parts: cheeks, chin, hair, teeth, tongue, neck, fingers, toes, knees, tummy, belly button (the last four body parts could be sung about during diapering). With older toddlers, add more detailed body parts such as eyebrows, shoulders, elbows, wrists, and ankles. With individual babies or toddlers, use their names.

Mirror Faces

Hold babies up in front of mirrors and point to their body parts, including eyes, ears, nose, mouth, cheeks, and chin. Always say the words as you point and use the baby's finger to point with. Point to your own features and name them as well. Do this frequently until the time when you say "Where are Susie's eyes?" and she actually points to them. Get excited about her mastery and show it by clapping or hugging and saying "Good!" Continue playing "Where are your eyes, nose, mouth, etc." game for several weeks after the baby has learned it and add new words like "tongue" or "teeth."

Paper Bag Faces

You'll need old newspapers; paper bags (lunch size); stapler; yellow, brown, black, or orange construction paper (cut into strips 1/4 inches wide); tape or glue; and pencils or markers.

Have children tear and crumple pieces of newspaper. Stuff the crumpled paper into the paper bags until they are three-fourths full. Fold the tops of the bags down and staple them shut. Press the bags between your hands to mold

them into round shapes. Have older children roll the stripes around a pencil or marker to make them curl. With glue, tape, or staples, attach the curled paper strips to the tops and backs of the bags for hair. Draw or glue features on the front of the bags for faces. Talk about what color to make the eyes and what shape the noses and mouths might be. Talk about how to make the faces look happy or sad.

You can do this project with mixed age groups since even toddlers love to tear and crumple paper and put things in bags. The older children can do the more complicated finishing features.

Variation: Paint the paper bag faces orange to become pumpkin faces for Halloween.

Magnetic Faces

Attach stickers of faces to pieces of magnetic tape and use them on refrigerators or dishwasher doors. Toddlers love playing with these magnets. Cut the magnetic tape close to the same size as the stickers to prevent the edges from tearing. Or draw faces on small felt rounds and attach them to magnetic tape.

Fe Fi Fo Fum

Fe fi fo fum	(*touch each finger with thumb—one finger for each syllable*)
See my fingers	(*hold up four fingers*)
See my thumb	(*hold up thumb*)
Fe fi fo fum	(*touch each finger with thumb again*)
Good-bye fingers	(*close fingers toward palm*)
Good-bye thumb	(*hide thumb under fingers*)

Baby

Here is baby's little head	(*hold up fist*)
That nods and nods and nods	(*bend fist up and down*)
Let's put him in a little bed	(*hold out other hand, curved like a cradle, and put fist into it*)
That rocks and rocks and rocks	(*rock fist cradled in other hand*)

What Does Baby Do?

This is what the baby does	
Clap, clap, clap	(*clap hands*)
This is what the baby does	
Play peek-a-boo	(*cover eyes and then remove hands on "boo"*)
This is what the baby does	
Creep, creep, creep	(*move fingers as if creeping—or creep fingers up infant's arm*)
This is what the baby does	
Sleep, sleep, sleep	(*lay head on hands*)

Playing Games with Baby

Babies from six or eight months to two years love interactive games that are variations on the peek-a-boo theme. The standard peek-a-boo as described in this verse is a favorite; here are some other versions to try:

- Put a handkerchief or cloth diaper over baby's face or your face and remove it as you gently say "boo." Repeat several times so the baby learns there is a surprise coming.

- Hide behind a chair, couch, or door (anywhere baby can't see you for a few seconds). Pop up and say "peek-a-boo." Again, repeat frequently to elicit a laughing response.

- Cover a teddy bear or other favorite toy with a cloth. Pretend to search for it saying, "Where's teddy?" several times. Remove the cloth saying, "There it is." Play this game frequently until baby removes the cloth and can find teddy without help.

- Attach ribbons to a teddy bear or other toy and hide it under a couch. Look for the toy and then pull the ribbon. As the toy emerges say, "There it is." Encourage the older infant or toddler to pull the ribbon to see what happens.

- This same activity can be used while the child is in a high chair. Tie a toy to the side of the high chair. The eight- to ten-month-old baby will undoubtedly toss the toy off the tray. Retrieve it by pulling on the ribbon while repeating, "There it is." (Supervise carefully.)

◆

The Creepy Mousie

Here comes the creepy, creepy, creepy mousie	(*say slowly while creeping two fingers up baby's arm*)
Right up to his little housie	(*tickle baby under chin on last word*)

Use with infants and repeat several times every day. This song will soon elicit delighted laughter of anticipation.

Baby Creeping
(*to the tune of "Frere Jacques"*)

Baby's creeping, baby's creeping
Round and round, round and round   (*imitate creeping in circles*)
Now he stops and looks around   (*stop and look around while on all fours*)
Picks some dust up from the ground   (*imitate picking up dust specs*)
Then plops down, then plops down   (*stretch out flat on ground*)

   You can sing this song with babies or have older children imitate baby actions—they love it!

Baby Grows (*Traditional*)

Five little fingers on this hand   (*hold up one hand with fingers extended*)
Five little fingers on that   (*hold up other hand*)
A dear little nose   (*point to nose*)
A mouth like a rose   (*pucker lips slightly and point to mouth*)
Two cheeks so tiny and fat   (*pretend to pinch cheeks*)
Two eyes, two ears   (*point to each*)
And ten little toes   (*wiggle toes and point to them*)
That's the way the baby grows   (*stretch arms up over head*)

So Big

Ask "How big is baby?" and then answer "So big" while lifting baby's arms over his head. Repeat this several times every day until baby lifts his arms up without your help when you say, "So big." Repeat with other phrases and accompanying actions such as play pat a cake, clap hands, and peek-a-boo. To describe actions to babies, repeat words and phrases. Ask questions and then repeat the answer with an accompanying action.

Baby Action Books

Take pictures of a baby's actions such as creeping, standing, playing peek-a-boo, doing "So big," and sleeping. Put the pictures into a small book (a small scrapbook, photo album, or Ziploc resealable bag). Label each picture with the child's name and the action each picture illustrates. Read the book together and emphasize the action words. See if the baby will imitate any of the actions described. Make individual books for each baby.

The Doggie Says Bow-Wow
(to the tune of "The Farmer in the Dell")

The doggie says bow-wow, the doggie says bow-wow
Hi-ho the merry-o, the doggie says bow-wow

The kitty says meow, the kitty says meow
Hi-ho the merry-o, the kitty says meow

The cow says moo, moo, the cow says moo, moo
Hi-ho the merry-o, the cow says moo, moo

The duck says quack, quack, the duck says quack, quack
Hi-ho the merry-o, the duck says quack, quack

Add additional animals as the children's attention and interest grows: the bird says tweet, tweet; the pig says oink, oink; the sheep says baa, baa.
You can also add: the baby says boo, hoo; the baby says bye, bye; or other words your toddlers are saying.

Animal Picture Books

"The Doggie Says Bow-Wow" is an excellent verse to chant as you look at animal picture books or as you hold up pictures of each animal. After using this song for several weeks, hold up an animal picture and see if the children know what that animal says. After the children know what each animal says, play games by trying to fool them and mixing up what the animal says (the dog says meow or the duck says moo, moo).

The Diapering Song *(to be sung while diapering)*
(to the tune of "Here We Go 'Round the Mulberry Bush")

This is the way we change your diapers
Change your diapers, change your diapers
This is the way we change your diapers
So early in the morning   *(sing as you carry child to changing area)*

First we take the wet one off
The wet one off, the wet one off   *(sing as you remove diaper; move baby's*
First we take the wet one off   *legs up to touch her chest a few times to*
So early in the morning   *the beat of the song)*

Now we put the dry one on
The dry one on, the dry one on
Now we put the dry one on
So early in the morning   *(sing as you get the new diaper in place)*

Now we snap up all the snaps
All the snaps, all the snaps
Snap and pull up the pants   *(sing during the finishing process and as*
So early in the morning   *you put baby down)*

Here We Go A Diapering
(loosely to the tune of "Here We Go A 'Wassailing")

Here we go a diapering
We do it every day
First we take the wet one off
And toss it all away
Then we wipe the little one
As with _____ legs we play   *(insert "his" or "her")*
And next the dry one
Covers up our precious _____ this way   *(insert baby's name)*

Repeat the first two lines at the end or use them as a chorus after each two-line verse.

As I'm Getting Bigger

Someone Special

I am someone special   *(point to self)*
And my name is all my own   *(point to name tag)*
No matter where I work or play   *(pretend to play with toys)*
My name is how I'm known   *(point to name tags)*

You are someone special   *(point to friends)*
And your name is all your own   *(point to friends' name tags)*
And when we play together   *(pretend to play)*
Our names are how we're known   *(point to each other's name tags)*

This is a good verse to use after making name tags during the getting acquainted process. Stress the uniqueness of each person's name and be sure to use first and last names for children whose first names are the same.

Name Tags

You'll need contact paper, various patterns or colors; blank address labels (or other gummed labels); stickers; scissors; markers; hole punch; and yarn.

Cut different shapes or objects (ball, star, triangle, square, house, car) from decorative contact paper. Stick blank address labels onto the shapes and print the child's name on the label. Have children decorate their name tag with stickers or their own designs or letters around their name.

Punch a hole in the top of the tag and string it with yarn to make a necklace. Have children wear the name tags for a few days and then use them as place cards at the table or to identify their cubbyhole, cot, things brought from home, or anything else needing a label.

Benjamin: A Name Story in Verse

This is a story about a boy named Benjamin
A name he thought just perfect for him
He liked it a lot
And never forgot
That he was Benjamin!

Then one day in the park playing with him
Was a boy who said he was Benjamin
Our Benjamin said, "That cannot be,
Benjamin belongs to me!
Can't you see that name is mine
You cannot have it any time!"

Then his mother explained he was Benjamin West
And this friend's parents also liked the name Benjamin best
So they named their boy Benjamin just the same
But the second part made it a different name.

So Benjamin West and Benjamin Brule
Played together often and soon went to nursery school
Where they met Benjamin Daly and Benjamin Brown
They all had the most popular first name in town.

Then their teacher said, "Boys, here is what we can do
To make sure each of your names is special for you.
Let's pick a nickname that is part of your name
And each one will be different, they won't be the same."

So one chose Ben and one became Benjie
One was called Jamie and one was B. B.
And each one said, "My nickname is perfect for me."
And sometimes they used Benjamin just the same
But they always added their own last name.

Name Plates

You'll need paper plates, a mirror, and markers or crayons.

Have the children draw a picture of themselves on a paper plate. Have them look in the mirror so they know their eye color, hair color, and shape of their nose. When they're done, print their name on the decorated plate. You can use these plates in games or when checking who is here. When they arrive, the children can put their plates on a bulletin board or in a shoe box saying, "We are here." You can also use the face plates as place cards for meals.

◆

A Nickname

Nathaniel James was called N. J.
Because Nathaniel was too hard to say.
Bartholomew Daniel became B. D.
To all his friends and family.
And even though they are almost grown
Those nicknames still are how they are known.

A nickname is a way you see
To make a name special for you or me,
It's usually short or it ends in "ie"
Like Ben or Jon or Robbie or Katie.

Or else, it tells something special about you
As "Curly" or "Freckles" or "Smiley" do.

A nickname can be fun to use
But you better be careful with the one you choose
'Cuz it may be a name you never lose!

A Book about Me

You'll need pictures of children (children can bring photos from home, draw their own, or cut out pictures from magazines); construction paper, scissors; markers or crayons; stapler; and Ziploc resealable bags (optional).

Make a book about each child and include topics such as my family, my house, my pets, things I like to do, things that I want to learn about, and things that interest me. Paste the photos from home onto construction paper or ask children to draw their own pictures. Staple them together to form a book. You can also use Ziploc resealable bags for these books. Staple, sew, or tie together three or four bags. Have the children draw or mount pictures on both sides of construction paper cut to fit inside the bags.

Let each child tell you about the pictures in her book. Write her own words on each page (simplify if necessary). Keep the books and read them often.

Make a similar book titled "Things I Like to Do at Child Care" (such as paint, work puzzles, build with blocks, play with friends; catalogs of child care equipment are good sources for pictures). Again, print the child's words or explanation on each page. Let the children take the books home and encourage parents to read them with their child.

A Box Full of Names

Collect and talk about items that are extensions of name tags. For example, driver's license, luggage tag, name bracelet or necklace, hospital identification bracelet, library card, credit card, social security card, monogram, name embossing machine, and name plate.

Feelings

Part of growing up I know
Is learning what my feelings show.
When I'm feeling happy
I often laugh and shout.
When I'm sad or lonely
I seem to mope and pout.
And when I'm very angry
Sometimes I cry and scream.
And when I'm feeling tired
I like to sit and dream.

Grumpy

Sometimes when I first wake up
I feel very grumpy and mad   (*make mad looking faces*)
Nothing seems to be just right
And the least little things make me sad   (*pretend to cry*)
But then I go to the kitchen
And eat some breakfast food   (*pretend to eat cereal*)
And then before I know it
I'm in a happy mood   (*make smiling faces*)

   Talk about how the children feel when they wake up. Do they feel the same when they wake up from a nap? When are some other times they might feel grumpy?

Feeling Faces

   You'll need magazines, scissors, paper, and glue.
   Have children find pictures in magazines that illustrate different feelings. Mount each picture on a piece of paper and talk about the pictures. Decide what feeling each depicts. Write a name for that feeling (such as angry, excited, scared, worried, surprised) on the picture. Discuss which feelings are happy, pleasant ones and which are sad, uncomfortable ones. Make up some stories about the pictures. Look at pictures that show children in various activities and decide which feeling picture would go with that activity picture.

◆

Brand New Shoes
(*to the tune of "Three Blind Mice"*)

Brand new shoes, brand new shoes
_____ has new shoes, _____ has new shoes   (*insert child's name*)
He likes to show off his tricky shoes   (*have child show something his shoes can do—jump, stamp, tap*)

We all can do it by ones and twos   (*children imitate trick*)
Those are wonderful tricky shoes
Brand new shoes, brand new shoes

Thinking about Shoes

Nothing is quite as exciting to young children as new shoes so remember to pay special attention to them as they appear. "Brand New Shoes" can be useful on such occasions. New shoes also create excellent opportunities to stretch vocabularies by talking about the different kinds of shoes children wear (tennis shoes, sandals, slippers, saddle shoes), the different names we call those shoes, and shoe parts (heels, laces, buckles, soles).

Talking about new shoes can lead to a discussion about what children or adults wear on their feet for special activities or work. Talk about the different types of boots, shoes for dancing and various sports, or footwear for the beach. Later, expand the discussion to foot coverings worn in different places or at different times. Show pictures or examples of different shoes such as wooden shoes, Japanese clogs, moccasins, or high top button-up boots. Think about materials used in the shoes and how shoes are made and repaired. Visit a shoe repair shop.

Shoes Galore!

Cut out pictures of different kinds of shoes and boots from catalogs and advertisements and cover them with clear contact paper. Use these shoe pictures for small group games and activities. In each case, spread out a large number of the shoe pictures. Have the children categorize them in some way and collect them in piles or boxes. There are many ways to categorize the shoes.

- What kind of shoe is it? Find all the children's tennis shoes, men's shoes, slippers, boots, high-heeled shoes and collect them in piles or boxes.

- Buckles and Bows. Find all the shoes that tie, all that close with Velcro fasteners, shoes that have buckles, and those with no fasteners.

- Who would wear it? Put out pictures of a man, woman, girl, boy, and baby. Find some shoes that each person would wear and place them by the corresponding picture.

- Find the pair. Pair up shoes that are alike.

- What color is it? Sort all the shoes by color.

The Birthday Cake

_____ has a birthday	*(insert birthday child's name and point to her)*
Let's all celebrate	
Here is her special cake	*(pretend to hold up cake)*
For us to decorate	
We'll cover it with frosting	*(pretend to frost cake)*
_____ she likes best	*(insert "chocolate" or "strawberry"—ask the child what kind)*
Put on this many candles	*(hold up number of fingers for age)*
Flowers and all the rest	*(pretend to make decorations)*
Light all the candles, see how they glow	*(pretend to light candles)*
Okay, _____, now it's your turn to blow	*(child blows and everyone claps)*

Birthday Activity

"The Birthday Cake" works well with a flannelboard birthday cake. Use the patterns to make a felt cake, candles, and decorations. As you say the verse, have the children take turns putting the appropriate pieces on the flannelboard. When the decorations are complete, have a child put the flames on the candles as if lighting the candles. Then have the birthday child pretend to blow out the candles.

Birthday Cake Dramatization

Another way to use "The Birthday Cake" is to act it out. The birthday child selects the children to be the candles and the decorations (such as flowers, clowns, or turtles). The birthday child stands with the adult as the children say the first verse. The adult draws a large imaginary circle on the floor to represent the cake.

For the second verse, the birthday child pretends to frost the cake; the candles come and stand on the cake; the decorations sit or squat on the cake; and the adult lights the candles. As the birthday child blows the candles out, they leave the cake. The adult and the birthday child then pretend to cut and serve the cake and everyone pretends to eat it.

My Teeth

There are teeth in my mouth
That are shiny and white   *(point to teeth)*
I brush them carefully morning and night   *(imitate brushing)*
They help me chew and keep my smile bright   *(make chewing motions and smile)*

Even though now they fit snug and tight
One of these days I may feel one wiggle
Then my tooth will get loose and jiggle and jiggle   *(pretend to wiggle a tooth)*
And my tooth will fall out and what do you know?   *(pretend to pull tooth out)*
In the very same spot a new tooth will grow

Big Mouth Tooth Collage

Cut large mouth shapes out of red construction paper and small, square teeth shapes from white paper. Let children glue the teeth on the mouth. Any arrangement works out fine, but children usually arrange them in two rows. Talk about the empty spaces in mouths when teeth begin to fall out or in babies before the teeth come in.

Invite a dentist to visit (or arrange a visit to a dental clinic). Ask the dentist to bring out X-rays of children's mouths showing the permanent teeth inside the gums underneath the existing teeth. Talk about how the new teeth pushing up make the "baby" teeth get loose and ready to fall out. Explain that this process happens naturally as children grow until they get all of their permanent teeth. Let them know that there's only one new set of permanent teeth in each child's mouth.

◆

My Body

A mouth to speak kind words each day   *(point to mouth)*
Two ears to listen to what others say   *(cup hands around ears)*
Two feet that help me run and play   *(move feet as if running)*
Two hands to put the toys away   *(pretend to pick up toys)*
Two eyes to see nice things to do   *(point to eyes)*
Two lips to smile the whole day through   *(point to lips and smile)*
A body that helps when there's work to be done   *(point to self)*
Makes a happy day for everyone   *(clap hands or pat self on back)*

Touch and Clap

Hands on shoulders, hands on knees   *(imitate all hand movements)*
Now hide them behind you, if you please!
Now touch your ears and then your nose
Hands on hips, then touch your toes.
Wave your hands up in the air
Now pat your sides then touch your hair.
Now let's clap 1-2-3-4
And all sit down upon the floor.

Body Collages

Have children look through magazines or newspapers and cut out people and body parts (faces in toothpaste ads, hair in shampoo ads, legs from tennis shoe ads, hands from lotion or jewelry ads, torso from clothing ads). Teachers may prefer to cut out the parts for younger children or let them tear them out. On a piece of paper, let the children paste the parts together to make body collages. They may combine body parts any way they like or draw on any missing parts. You can use this activity as a conversation starter to talk about bodies and how they are put together.

Find out what else children want to learn about their bodies. Read the "Let's Read and Find Out" Science Books, which describe various body parts and functions. Titles in the series include *A Drop of Blood* by Paul Showers (1989); *Straight Hair, Curly Hair* by Augusta Goklin (1966); and *What Happens to Hamburger* by Paul Showers (1985).

◆

Hinges *(Traditional)*

I'm all made of hinges
So everything bends   *(make bending movements)*
From the top of my head
Way down to my ends.
I've hinges in front   *(bend forward)*
I've hinges in back   *(bend back)*
I'm glad I've got hinges
Or else I would crack!

Discuss with the children various body "hinges" otherwise known as joints, such as wrist, elbow, neck, ankle, and knee. Contrast the immovable parts that sometimes crack (the bones) with the movable parts (the joints) that make it possible to move.

Two by Two

Fat thumbs, fat thumbs	
What can you do?	*(hold out two fists)*
Pop up, pop down	*(pop up both thumbs)*
Two by two	*(wiggle thumbs)*

   Repeat for each finger: pointer finger, middle finger, ring finger, little finger. Pop up each finger in turn and pull it in to make a fist again.

Whole hands, whole hands	
What can you do?	*(hold out two fists)*
Clap, clap, clap, clap	
Two by two	*(clap hands)*

Movable Doll Pattern

   Use the pattern to cut out body parts for a doll. Assemble the doll using brass fasteners to attach the arm and leg parts and head to the torso. Encourage the children to name each of the joints as you assemble and play with the doll.

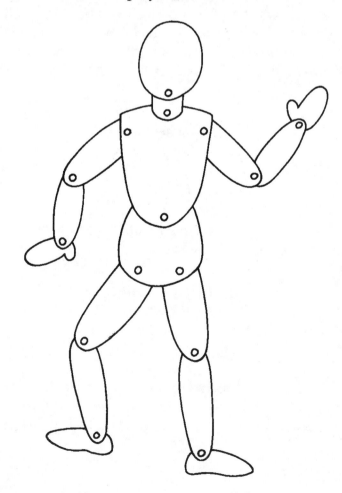

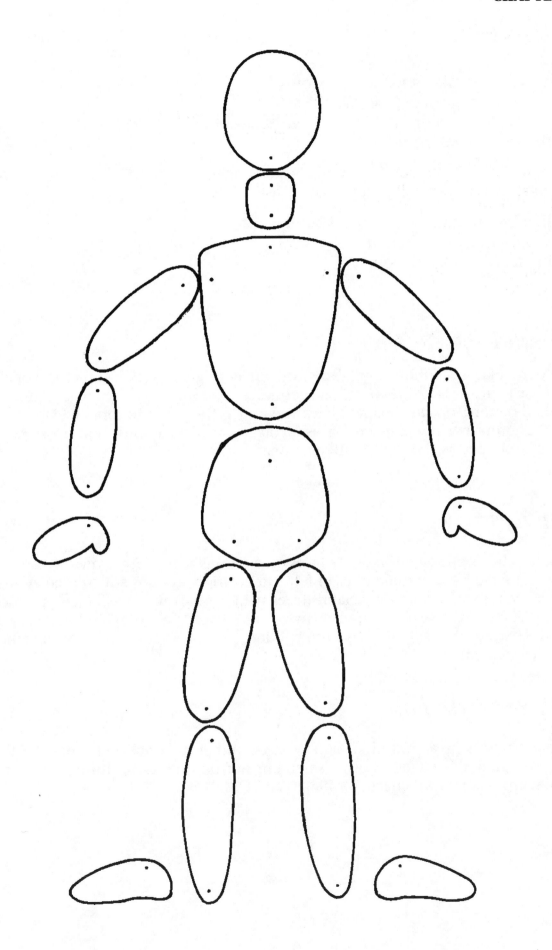

Faces

Some faces are oval, some faces are round
Some faces are fat, some faces are thin
Some faces are shades of red, yellow, white, or brown
Sometimes faces wear a jolly grin
And sometimes they wear a frown.

Some faces belong to children
Who live in Japan or Peru
In Russia or Turkey or Thailand
And one face belongs to you.

Face Puppets

   Locate the places mentioned in "Faces" on a map or globe and find pictures of children from those countries (airlines or travel agents are good sources for pictures). Mount individual pictures on small paper plates and attach the plates to tongue blades. Use the puppets as props when you recite "Faces." You can also make smile and frown face puppets or puppets with faces of different shapes.

Felt Faces

   Cut large circles out of felt to use as faces on a flannelboard. Use brown, cream, yellow, and tan colors for faces. From scraps of felt, cut a variety of different colored eyes and hair and a variety of shapes for facial features (wide or narrow noses, open or closed mouths). You could also use cut-out pictures from magazines and glue Velcro fasteners or felt to the back of these pieces. Have the children put together different arrangements of features to create faces.

Faces You Can Eat

   Make faces using bread rounds or buns. Use peanut butter or cheese spread for the face. Add raisins, grapes, bananas, or other small bits of fruit for facial features. Decorate with licorice strips or shredded cheese for hair.

Rock Faces

Paint faces on rocks using round, oval, oblong, or triangular shaped rocks at least 2 1/2 to 3 inches wide. When dry, paint over the rocks with clear nail polish. Display your rock faces by standing them up in egg cartons.

Visit a sculpture exhibit that includes faces. Show the children pictures of sculptures by Leonardo da Vinci or Michelangelo or of the famous rock group at Mount Rushmore.

Shadow Dance

See the five people all in a row	*(hold up five fingers on one hand)*
See their shadows facing just so	*(hold second hand parallel to first)*
The first one bends and says, "Hello"	*(bend thumb)*
And then its shadow also bends low	*(bend other thumb)*
The next one starts to twirl around	*(twirl finger on first hand)*
And so does its shadow without a sound	*(corresponding finger does same)*
Whatever the first person tried to do	*(fingers on first hand make different motions)*
The second one said, "I'll do it, too."	*(fingers on second hand repeat motions)*

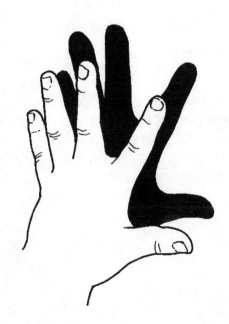

Shadow Games

Divide the children into pairs. One child is the shadow and imitates whatever movements his partner makes (raising arms, jumping, waving). Let each child have a chance to be the initiator and the shadow.

CHAPTER TWO: From Home to School or Child Care

Introduction

Leaving home is a big step for any person. Many professionals have written about how adolescents and young adults make this change. These professionals recognize that leaving home is a big transition because of the physical separation involved. For the young child, going off to school or child care is just as big (if not bigger) a transition. The young child is physically separating from a familiar environment and beloved people, even if only for a few hours.

A young child attending a new school or child care experiences all the feelings associated with being in a strange place: not knowing what to do, not knowing what to expect from those around you, and feeling a sense of loss. Furthermore, the young child must confront this separation without a base of experience or the cognitive understanding that this new place is okay and mom or dad really will return.

Young children are also limited in their abilities to integrate the two experiences and explain things about one setting to the significant people in the other. Finger plays, poems, and simple activities can help young children practice and act out the process of separation, acquire ideas about what to expect in the new setting, and offer ways to share information about each setting.

Today, child care or early education comes in multiple forms and a large variety of settings. These include not only the traditional nursery school, child care center, or family child care home, but also parent and child programs, preschool play groups, tiny tots gym groups, recreational programs of every variety, and drop-in groups. The physical spaces also vary from a traditional home or classroom to an elementary school, park and recreation center, health club, or shopping mall. With a little imagination and a few word substitutions, most of the songs in this section can be adapted to fit any program type.

Also included is a list of ways to help children get started in child care, which you may want to share with parents. Suggestions on how to communicate with parents are at the end of this section.

Going to School/Child Care

A Hug and a Kiss
(to the tune of "Here We Go 'Round the Mulberry Bush")

I give my mother a hug and a kiss
A hug and a kiss, a hug and a kiss
I give my mother a hug and a kiss
When I go to school each morning   *(or use the name of the home or center)*

 Sing additional verses for other important people such as father, sister, brother, grandma; or of things, such as teddy bear, doll, stuffed animal. Let the children tell you who they kiss good-bye before they go to school.

I give my mother a hug and a kiss
A hug and a kiss, a hug and a kiss,
I give my mother a hug and a kiss
When she picks me up each day   *(or When I go home each day)*

 Repeat with other family members.

Down at the Center
(to the tune of "Down by the Station")

Down at the center, early in the morning
See all the children hurry through the door
See the busy parents scurry to and fro
Hug, hug, kiss, kiss, off to work they go

Here at the center, later in the afternoon
See all the parents hurry through the door
See the busy children with so much to show
Hug, hug, kiss, kiss, now it's home we go

 Singing the first verse of this song every day for parents and children during their first few weeks and again after vacations can help everyone see this sometimes painful separation process as a daily routine. The song can become part of a separation ritual. Add the second verse, if you wish, either in the morning or as a ritual to end the day. For those who come on a school bus, sing this version of the same song:

Down at the corner, early in the morning
See the parents and kids waiting in a row
Here comes the school bus, wait until it stops for us
Kiss, kiss, wave, wave, off to school we go

Going to School
(to the tune of "Here We Go 'Round the Mulberry Bush")

This is the way I go to school
Go to school, go to school
This is the way I go to school
So early in the morning

I ride on the bus to go to school
Go to school, go to school
I ride on the bus to go to school
With Mommy every morning

I drive in the car to go to school
Go to school, go to school
I drive in the car to go to school
With Daddy every morning

Let the children tell you how they come to school and with whom. For additional verses, use all the different ways the children come to school (walk, in trains, taxis, school buses, carpools) and all the different people who accompany them (grandparents, friends, baby-sitters).

Imitate the actions associated with the different means of transportation such as pretending to drive the car, bounce up and down on the bus, and walk.

Flannelboard Fun

"Going to School" can also be used as a flannelboard activity. Make felt cutouts of the vehicles (school bus, car, train, taxi, city bus) and people to use as you sing about them. Include cutouts of a home and the center. Another possibility is to cut pictures of all these vehicles and people from magazines. Mount small pieces of felt on the back of each picture to use on the flannelboard.

In either case, as you sing this song, have the child who is telling how she came to school select the appropriate pictures to put on the flannelboard. You might also pause in your singing to let the child tell you about anything special or interesting that happened on the trip to child care. Let several children have a chance to tell or sing about how they came to school each day. Be sure that you let everyone have a turn over the course of a few days.

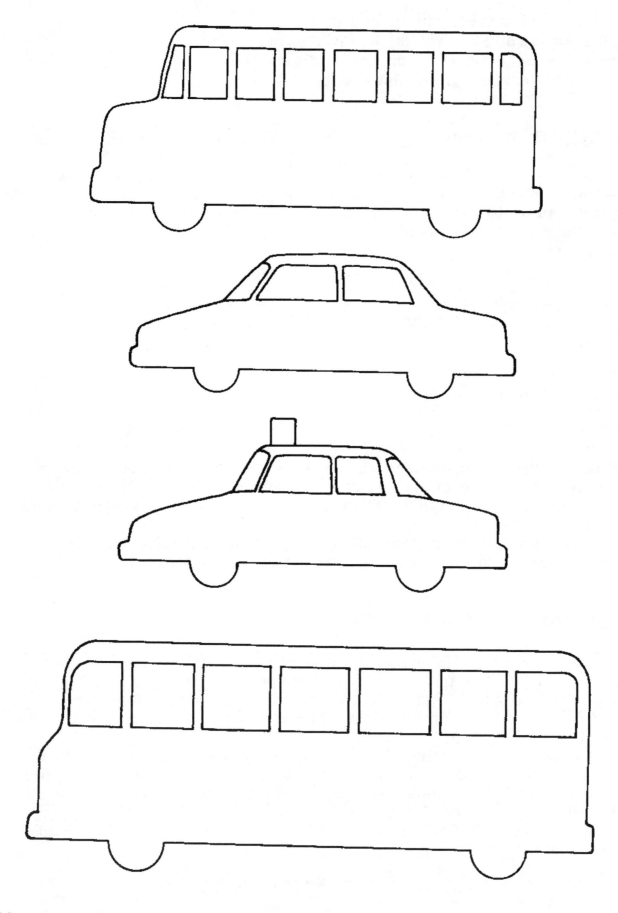

Things We Do at School
(to the tune of "Here We Go 'Round the Mulberry Bush")

This is the way we build with blocks
Build with blocks, build with blocks
This is the way we build with blocks
So early in the morning   *(imitate building)*

This song and technique is easily adapted to describe what goes on at school or child care as well as to establish routines. Additional verses: do a puzzle, read some books, ride our bikes, pick up the toys, eat our lunch, take a nap (imitate all the actions).

Off to School or Child Care

Slip off your jacket   *(pretend to take off jacket)*
Put down your toys and books   *(put thing down)*
Open up the locker   *(open door motion)*
Hang things on the hooks   *(pretend to hang up jacket)*

Now we all are ready
Off to class we go   *(march around the room)*
We'll listen to our teachers   *(sit down in front of teacher)*
There's a lot to learn, you know   *(pretend to open book)*

Many verses can be adapted for home or other child care setting by altering a few words. Family child care providers can substitute "closet" for "locker" or "work" for "class." The verses can also be personalized by substituting names for the generic word "teacher."

Going to Child Care Game

To create a "Going to Child Care" game, you'll need a 12" x 18" piece of tagboard or a file folder, markers or crayons, and about twelve 3" x 5" file cards.

Draw a path on the tagboard or file folder. Divide this path into squares for moving playing pieces forward. At the start of the path, draw a house and label it "Home." At the end of the path, draw a building and label it with the name of the child care setting. Along the path at certain spaces put pictures of items that are part of the getting ready process (clothes for dressing, a toothbrush, breakfast food, a car, traffic lights).

Cut the file cards in half to make playing cards. On most of the cards write either "1," "2," or "3" and draw a corresponding number of dots. On the remaining cards, draw pictures and directions for special actions to be taken. For example, draw a picture of a car and write, "Car Trouble—Go back to car." Draw a toothbrush and write, "Go to Toothbrush." Draw socks and shoes and write, "Can't find shoes—Go to clothes." On a few other cards, draw either a red or green color dot (for a traffic light). For these cards, the children go to the nearest traffic light. If the card is red, they lose a turn; if it is green, they get another turn.

To play, have children choose player pieces (thimbles, rocks, erasers, buttons). Have them pick cards and move along the path according to the numbers or instructions on the cards.

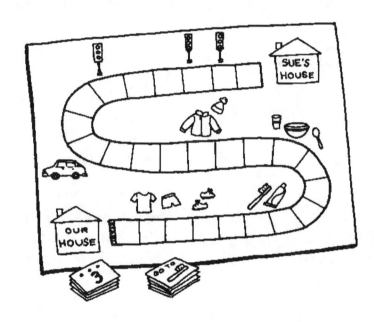

Night and Morning *(Traditional)*

This little boy is going to bed	*(first finger of right hand on palm of left)*
Down on the pillow he lays his head	*(thumb of left hand is pillow)*
Wraps himself in the covers tight	*(fingers of left hand close)*
This is the way he sleeps all night	
Morning comes, he opens his eyes	
Back with a toss the covers fly	*(fingers of left hand open)*
Up he jumps, is dressed and away	*(right index finger up and hopping away)*
Ready to go to school today	

The Clock *(Author unknown)*

Tick-tock, tick-tock,
Listen to the clock.   *(hand to ear)*
What does it say
All the day?
It says tick-tock
Tick-tick-tock.   *(swing arms as a pendulum)*

It tells us when we go to school,
And when we go to bed;
But we must listen   *(hand to ear)*
To its talk
Of tick-tock
Tick-tick-tock.   *(swing arms as a pendulum)*

Getting Acquainted with a Child Care Home or Center

At School or Child Care

When everyone is singing,
That's what I like to do.   *(pretend to sing)*
And when they're drawing pictures,
I draw pictures, too.   *(pretend to draw pictures)*

When it's time to work with toys,
I build a house of blocks.   *(pretend to build with blocks)*
When they say, "Put toys away,"
I put them in a box.   *(pretend to put toys away)*

When someone asks for help,
I always say "I will."   *(point to self)*
And when it's time for "Quiet please"
I'm very, very still.   *(put index finger to lips)*

This is a good poem for beginning a group time. The last verse might not always hold true, but repeating it may inspire some like actions.

Around and Around Our Room We Go

Around and around our room we go
Walking fast, walking slow,
Look around you, what do you know?
Walk to your favorite place, just so.

   Repeat this verse using different action words, such as jump, skip, tiptoe, and slide. Have the children go to different parts of the room or house (jump to the kitchen, skip to the window).

Our House Has Many Rooms
(to the tune of "The Farmer in the Dell")

Our house has many rooms, our house has many rooms
Hi-ho the merry-o, our house has many rooms

Our house has a family room, our house has a family room
Hi-ho the merry-o, we play there you know

   Additional verses: Our house has a bedroom. . .We nap there you know; Our house has a kitchen. . .We cook there you know.
   Adapt this song to fit your own setting to acquaint the children with what will go on in each space, such as basement, backyard, and laundry area.

Our Center Has Many Rooms
(variation for centers or schools; to the tune of "The Farmer in the Dell")

Our center has many rooms, our center has many rooms
Hi-ho the merry-o, our center has many rooms

Our center has a lunchroom, our center has a lunchroom
Hi-ho the merry-o, we eat there you know

   Additional verses: Our center has a gym. . .We run and play there you know. Use whatever labels you use for the various areas, corners, or rooms you have in the center. Include the office, library, music room (or corner), and toddler room.

A Big Book about Child Care

Make up a book about your child care setting. Take a picture of each room in your home or center that the children use as well as extra spaces, such as the backyard or playground, basement, office, and bathrooms. Mount each picture on a separate piece of paper and staple the pages together.

As you show the pictures to the children, talk about each room. Describe its color, decorations, and objects found there. Ask the children what they like to do there, any special rules for that area, and anything else they think of. Ask them what they don't like about a particular room or area.

On one or two pages, write some general rules or things to remember at child care, such as procedures for cleaning up, putting papers in special places, shelves for toys from home, where children put their clothes, and how many children can play in some places at one time. Ask the children what they would like to include in their "Book about Child Care." Add to it from time to time as the children master more procedures, such as care of art materials or rules for care of pets or plants, routines for meals, snacks, and naps. Let the children decorate some of the pages of the book.

Read the book frequently and at the children's request. It is especially good to reread the book after a child has been away because of a vacation or illness or when new children come. It will also be fun to read as the year goes by to see what changes have been made in any room or area and what additions you need to make to your book.

◆

Clean Up Time
(to the tune of "Jingle Bells")

Clean up time, clean up time
Clean up all the toys
Trucks and cars, dolls and blocks
We're working girls and boys

Clean up time, clean up time
Time to put away
Trucks and cars, dolls and blocks
Were lots of fun today

Helpers

Little fingers, little fingers
Helpers all are we   *(hold hands up and wiggle fingers)*
We pick up toys, and hang up clothes
Busy as can be   *(imitate picking up items)*

Clean Up

We all worked together
At school today
We picked up our blocks   *(pretend to pick up blocks)*
And put them away.   *(pretend to put them away)*

We picked up our puzzles and games galore
We cleaned up the tables   *(pretend to wipe tables)*
And swept up the floor.   *(pretend to sweep floors)*

Can I Play?

Repeating poems and finger plays is a helpful way to encourage helping behavior and teach daily routines and schedules. You can also use picture charts of the day's activities and job charts or necklaces with pictures of the jobs to help children learn the routines and procedures at child care.

Use clothespins with pictures of jobs or play activities mounted on them to help children select and remember things they are supposed to do at certain times. Children wear the clothespins on their shirt and place them on a small clotheslines (at the their level) when finished.

Clothespin picture cards of activity choices can help set physical limits on the number of children who can choose particular activities. If there are only four cards for the block area or playhouse corner or two for the Lego building blocks and one for a brand-new toy, the assignment of these activities is handled by self-selection. The children choose a picture card and wear it while working or playing in a particular area. Adult direction can be quite minimal, primarily reminding the children to put the cards back when they are finished so others may choose them. Here is an example of one type of job chart:

A Helper's Chart

To make your own helper's chart, you'll need tagboard, markers or crayons, and clothespins.

On the tagboard, write down all of the jobs that need to be done in your setting (set the table, water the plants, feed the fish). On each clothespin, write down the name of a child. Move the clothespins in rotation along the chart and clip them to the job each child does that day. One teacher used an octopus on her chart. In each of its eight arms, the octopus held a different job and a picture of the job. You could use a flowerpot with flowers for each job, a fruit bowl, or a clown holding balloons.

Magic Words *(author unknown)*

Putting on your coat, or tying your cap
Or zipping a zipper, or snapping a snap.
If you want someone to help you with a task
Say, "Please help me" when you ask.
When your coat is done, and your cap is tied,
And you're all ready to go outside
Before you go, remember to say,
"Thank you" to the person who helped you today.

The Power of Positive Thinking

Every day is a busy day
With time for work and time for play
Taking turns with all these toys
Trying to help other girls and boys
We're all getting better at waiting awhile
And remembering people like us to smile
Now one more thing we should try to be:
Careful with things, and you and me.   *(point to others)*

Knowledge of success and recognition of positive growth is helpful in encouraging its continuation. Poems like the above or songs such as "Helping" go a lot further to acknowledge and encourage positive behavior than lengthy adult discussions or punishments for inappropriate behavior.

Helping
(to the tune of "If You're Happy and You Know It")

If you helped another child, pat your back
If you helped another child, pat your back
If you're helpful and you know it
Then your smile will clearly show it
If you're helpful and you know it, pat your back

Additional verses: If you're careful with our toys, clap your hands; If you asked for turns at playing, shake your head.

We Helped Today

Write stories about the things children did to help others. Include the child's name and what he or she did to help.

Make a booklet or chart that lists things that make people happy and things that make them sad. Use a smile or a frown face for each category. Let the children tell you what to write in each section. Go over the lists frequently to remind the children about helping behaviors at child care.

Getting Acquainted with Each Other

Getting to Know You
(to the tune of "Where Is Thumbkin?")

Teacher:
>   Where is _____? Where is _____?   *(insert child's first and last names)*

Child:
>   Here I am, here I am

Teacher and other children:
>   How are you today, _____?   *(repeat first name)*

Child:
>   Very well I thank you

Teacher and other children:
>   _____ is here, _____ is here   *(repeat first name)*

Continue singing until all the children have had their names called. Sing this at the beginning of the year to help children get to know each other. For the children who are absent, the whole group responds, "He's not here, he's not here" after the teacher's question. Try to keep the song moving along quickly so the children don't lose interest. If necessary, separate into a small group with each staff person leading a group and divide up your attendance lists. Your group can also sing this song for name recognition alone without using it for attendance purposes, thereby omitting the absent children.

How Are You?
(to the tune of "If You're Happy and You Know It")

Good morning, _____   *(insert child's first and last names)*
How are you?   *(encourage each child to wave, smile, or do something to respond)*

Good morning, _____   *(repeat name)*
How are you?
How are you this _____ day   *(fit in the proper description: sunny, cloudy, rainy)*

We're so glad you've come to play
Good morning, _____   *(repeat name)*
How are you?

You can use the whole verse for each child in the beginning of the year and later condense it using one line for each child and singing "Good morning, everybody" for the last line.

Roll It

Name games are useful in helping children learn each other's names. "Roll It" is a simple game to use after the children know at least a few names of other children.

Have the children sit in a circle with one child in the center holding a ball. The child in the center calls the name of a child around the circle and rolls the ball to her. That child catches the ball, calls out the center child's name, and rolls the ball back. The center child then gives the ball to another child who will be the new child in the center. (The center child may roll the ball to several different children before choosing a replacement.)

Name Chant

Oh, here we are together, together, together.
Oh, here we are together all sitting on the floor.
Here's _____ and _____ and _____ and _____.   *(put in children's names)*
Oh, here we are together all sitting on the floor.

Make a Welcoming Tree

Bring in a large tree branch with several limbs or smaller branches. Plant it in a large coffee can filled with sand or plaster of Paris. Mount pictures of children on small, round plastic lids. Poke a hole in the top of the lid, string yarn through it, and tie. Hang the pictures on tree branches and put the tree in the center of the circle when you sing "Here We Go 'Round the Welcoming Tree."

Here We Go 'Round the Welcoming Tree
(to the tune of "Here We Go 'Round the Mulberry Bush")

(refrain)
Here we go 'round the welcoming tree
The welcoming tree, the welcoming tree
Here we go 'round the welcoming tree
So early in the morning

This is the way we smile at our friends
Smile at our friends, smile at our friends
This is the way we smile at our friends
So early in the morning   *(repeat refrain)*

Additional verses: This is the way we wave, shake hands, throw kisses, wink, nod. Children hold hands and walk around the tree while singing the refrain. Stop and imitate actions for the verses.

Friends at Play

One little child with nothing to do	(hold up one finger)
Found a friend to play with	
And then there were two	(hold up two fingers)
Two little children, playing happily	
Along came another and then there were three	(hold up three fingers)
Three little children playing grocery store	
Along came a customer and then there were four	(hold up four fingers)
Four little children with cars and trikes to drive	
Along came a friend in a wagon, and then there were five.	(hold up all five fingers)

This Little Child

This little child scraped his knee	(hold up and wiggle thumb)
This little child said, "Oh, dear me!"	(hold up first finger)
This little child laughed and was glad	(hold up second finger)
This little child cried and was sad	(hold up third finger)
But this little child so helpful and good	(wiggle fourth finger)
Ran for the teacher as fast as he could.	(move pinkie away fast)

Be sure to discuss the appropriate and inappropriate ways to respond when people get hurt.

One Little Friend
(to the tune of "One Elephant Went Out to Play")

One little friend went out to play
Out to the park on a summer day
He had such enormous fun
He called for another little friend to come.

Additional verses: Two little friends, three little friends, etc. Children form a circle, one player walks around the inside of the circle as everyone sings the verse. At the appropriate line, he selects another child to join him. Repeat, increasing number of friends.

Getting Acquainted Picture Games

Take photos of each child or have them bring a current snapshot of themselves from home. Gather photos of staff members. Play a variety of games using the pictures.

- Spread out all the pictures. Have children try to find their own picture. (Help those who can't.)

- Add music and play musical chairs. Put each child's picture on a chair and start the music. When the music stops, children find the chair with their picture. Mix the pictures up and repeat.

- Divide the children into two groups. Give each child in one group a picture of a child in the other group. Play music and have the children march around. When the music stops, have each child with a picture find the person in that picture. When they find their partner be sure they tell each other their names. Switch groups and repeat the game.

- Divide the group into pairs. Spread out pictures and have each pair find the pictures of each other. Be sure the children tell each other their names when they find their pictures.

- Play "Who Is It?" Teacher describes a child to the group. The group tries to guess who it is and the child who guesses and gives the right name finds the picture of that child. Notice what is different from the picture (clothes are different but it's still the same person). Include teachers in your descriptions.

An Ode to Teachers and Caregivers

"Teacher, Teacher, Joe took my toy!"   *(substitute your name if you wish)*
"Tell him to ask you like a big boy."
"Teacher, Teacher, they won't let me play."
"Take them these cars or would you like some clay?"
"Teacher, Teacher, tie my shoe!"
"Teacher, Teacher, what can I do?"
So many questions and demands each day,
But you always know just what to say!
And now another day is through,
"Teacher, Teacher, we love you!"

From Child Care to Home

Lonesome

If I miss my Mommy   *(or Daddy)*
I know what to do
I look at her picture
And say, "I love you."

If you don't have individual photo albums available, make a large mural with photos of the children's parents.

Comfort Me

An excellent idea to ease the transition to child care is to encourage parents to help their child prepare a small photo album filled with pictures of family members, pets, and favorite toys. (Parents can make one to send with toddlers.) When children feel lonesome or unfamiliar, they can browse through this form of portable security, and the teacher or caregiver can give added support while learning all about the important things in each child's life. These photo albums can help children who are having difficulty with the transition to child care and again after vacations, illnesses, or any extended absence, or just on "Blue Mondays."

Helping Your Child Get Started in Child Care

Starting a child in a day care arrangement is a big change for both parent and child. It can be an emotionally upsetting experience for both. With a little thoughtful planning in advance, however, the transition can be made easier for everyone.

- If you will be going back to work, get your baby used to other people right from the start. Have relatives or friends occasionally care for the baby.

- Allow plenty of time to find the best arrangement (the younger the child the harder it may be to find care).

- Spend time with your child at the child care site before you leave your child there. Make as many short visits in advance as you and the caregiver can arrange.

- If possible, start part-time child care a few days before you have to go to work. That way, your child's first stays can be shorter and you have more time to get her settled in before you get busy.

- Try to feel and act positively toward the new experience; your child picks up on your feelings and actions.

- Talk to your child (in age-appropriate ways) about *specific* things in the child care center or home that may appeal to him. Avoid broad sweeping statements like "You'll just love it" or "You'll have a wonderful time." The child needs more concrete ideas to relate to. Talk about the settings, routines, and caregiver in ways that compare and relate to things he already knows ("They eat lunch in the kitchen, too" or "They have little tables to eat lunch at").

- Before your child begins, practice the new routine through dramatic play. Pretend to go to the center or home, hang up child's coat, choose something appealing to play with, eat a snack, take a rest, use the bathroom. Be sure to act out Mom or Dad picking up the child at the end of the day.

- Consider making a photo album for your child to take to child care, showing family friends, favorite toys, and activities. The album might be just the "security blanket" your child needs. Also, bring along that real security blanket if your child has one.

- Read books about beginning "school" or child care to your child. A good one to start with is *Will I Have a Friend?* by Miriam Cohen (Collier, 1989). For you and older preschoolers you might try *A Child Goes to School* by Sara Bonnett Stein (Doubleday, 1978). You might make up your own storybook using your own child, the real setting, caregiver, children, and materials in it.

- You might consider getting a special toy or animal that stays at child care. Going to child care becomes going to see "Care Bear" and leaving is saying, "Good-bye, Care Bear, see you tomorrow." A new toy or animal is especially useful with older infants or toddlers.

- Remember that your child will approach the transition in her own characteristic style; if that style is usually to be upset with new situations, tears may be part of the normal adjustment to child care. It is helpful to develop a routine way to say good-bye and then follow it. Be sensitive to your child's feelings and accept those feelings, but don't feel you have to act differently as a result. Call later to see if all is well.

- Stay in close communication with the teacher, center director, or child care provider to work out a satisfactory plan before and during the transition.

How to Talk to Your Child about Child Care

Talking to your child about what goes on during the day while you are away can be a real challenge. First of all, children typically don't communicate a lot about what they have done. They are most apt to answer your "What did you do today?" questions with "Nothing," or "Play," simple words that they can think of immediately. If you think back to your own school days, you may have answered your parent's questions in the same way. First of all, the "What did you do today?" question is too big. Second, how can a child begin to explain the complicated issues of who said what to whom and all the varied ideas and activities he had pursued that day?

To help build some communication, start with narrow questions about specific things that might take place during the day. Let your child expand on that subject as he remembers something or senses your interest in the little details of the day. Listed are some conversation starter questions to use as you wish.

- What kind of puzzles do they have at your school? Which are the hard (or easy) ones?

- Does anyone build with blocks? Who? What do they like to make the most? Are there other things to build with? What kinds of things do you build?

- Did you hear a story today? What was it about, do you remember?

- How high up the climber do the children climb? Who likes to climb the most?

- Does anyone play pretend games while on the climber (or in the house, or using the blocks)?

- What kinds of things do you use in the sandbox?

Notice that all of these questions have a general activity focus producing less pressure on the child to remember his own activities. They also may feel less intrusive into what children often consider their private life. With this approach, chances are you'll hit on something your child did and you can learn more about his personal reactions by expanding your questions in that direction.

To encourage continuing conversation, show interest in finding out more by asking more questions, repeating the last words your child said, or responding in some positive way such as "that sounds like lots of fun." Remember, if you only respond to or show interest in problem areas, such as "someone took my toy" or "they wouldn't let me play," those are the kind of statements you'll continue to hear. Children quickly learn the kinds of things that interest you and repeat those things as their part in encouraging conversation. How you respond to negative comments can help your child learn social skills and will continue the efforts we start here.

Some possible responses to "complaints":

- Oh, that's too bad. What did you do when that happened?

- Can you tell _____ not to bother you, that you don't like it? He may just want to play with you.

- Maybe you should tell _____ you will give him the toy when you are finished, if he asks you.

- Maybe you can ask your teacher for some cars to use with the blocks and see if the children will build a garage for your cars. Sometimes it helps if you think up new ideas. Maybe you could just start using some of the blocks the others are not using and build your own building near theirs.

- Your teachers can help you if the children get too rough or when you have trouble. Just ask them.

Please tell the teacher or caregiver if your child has an unusual number of complaints so they can work together to help your child adjust successfully to his group.

What Did You Do Today?

If you ask your child
"What did you do today?"
Don't be surprised
If she has nothing to say.

The question's so big
Where should she begin?
It's hard to remember everything!
Better say, "Nothing"; that's easy to say
It really was too busy and complicated a day.

For better information
It's best to say,
"Did you hear a story
or paint today"?
Then help her remember what it was about
And before you know it, more things will pour out.
So ask for specifics about things that we do
It will be much easier for your child to tell you.

If you want to know what those things might be
Look at the daily plan on the wall and see
Or ask and we'll be happy to say
How many different things we did today!

The hand out "How to Talk to Your Child about Child Care" offers one approach to improving parent/child communication. The poem, "What Did You Do Today?" which also should be given to parents, may be more effective in communicating that message. The following activity gives you a role in encouraging communication.

Things We Liked Today

Write a summary of the day's most-enjoyed activities with the children. This can be done around snack time in the afternoon in a very conversational way. Include individual names and their comments. This will help children remember some of the many things they did that day. By posting this list in a handy spot where parents will see it, you offer parents some very helpful conversation starters. (If there is different staff with the children when they awaken from their nap, do the activity as a transition to lunch or as a preparation for naps.)

Verses, such as those following, can also get a message across to parents more effectively than other techniques.

The Locker Limerick *(author unknown)*

There was a young child at school,
Who at naptime woke up in a pool.
Teacher sought a dry pair
But the locker was bare
And so the poor child was too!

Parent Reminders

Wednesday's the day I take a trip
If you remember to sign this slip.

   Or used for big signs:

Check inside this little box
If you are missing any socks.

   or vice versa:

If you have extra mittens or socks
Put some in this special box!

Not only kittens
Lose their mittens.   *(for a display or box of lost mittens)*

If you can help us repair or sew
We would really like to know.

If you have to wait awhile
We hope you can spare a smile.

CHAPTER THREE: Things that Work in the World

Introduction

Helping children make sense of their world is one of the major goals of early childhood education and should be part of the ideas and activities we bring to our children's early learning experiences. Children's natural curiosity about the things in their world give us an ideal beginning.

We as caregivers and early childhood teachers, however, may be fearful of trying to explain the high tech world in which we live. Indeed, we may not know most of the answers to the questions children raise. In our avoidance of these questions and our failure to include any acknowledgement of technology, we inadvertently may dampen our children's curiosity and desire to know more. This is an extremely unfortunate by-product since our major goal should be stimulating our children's interest in learning. It is not important that we actually know how to explain various technologies. It is more important that we recognize that there are many interesting things to think and learn about in our world. It is important that we stimulate some speculation and discussion about our world and that we demonstrate how to find out more through the use of books, libraries and community resources.

The verses and activities in this section offer an opportunity to raise some questions and encourage children's observation and awareness of today's technology. We also hope that they will support children in their drive to understand and make sense of their world.

Machines Around the World

What Makes Things Go?

The thing about machines that I don't quite know,
Is what it is that makes them go!
Mother says it's electricity
But what makes that I cannot see.
I know it comes through wires and such
Things like cords, plugs, and sockets I mustn't touch.

But there's a wonderful little car I know
You just rub the wheels fast to make it go!
I wonder how that car of mine
Is anything like a power line?

Horsepower

On farms and in towns a long time ago
Horses pulled things to make them go.
They trotted fast to turn the wheels
Of the things they pulled behind their heels.
"Horsepower" we called the force they created
Now in engines that power is generated
Motors turn wheels to make things go
And even send power to our house, you know.

Powerful Ideas

Both "What Makes Things Go?" and "Horsepower" are good conversation starters that can lead to a discussion about what makes things work. Let the children discuss their ideas of how things work and see what questions they raise in thinking about this topic. Other ideas to try:

- Talk about the words associated with electricity (plugs, sockets, cords, wires, battery, shock, friction), what they mean, and why we don't touch some of these things.

- Show how a flashlight works. Take the batteries out and see what happens. Explain that batteries are the smallest form of electric generators. Look at different sizes of batteries and talk about what they are used for—ranging from tiny flashlight or watch batteries to more powerful car batteries.

- Make a small electric circuit board. You'll need pegboard, a battery, wire, switches, and a light or bell. (Directions can be found in encyclopedias or simple science books.) Provide screwdrivers and small pliers so children can take apart and reassemble the circuit board as often as they wish. Provide enough pegboards, wires, batteries, and switches to make additional circuit boards if the children are interested. Notice what happens when different size batteries are used.

- Visit a power plant and show the children the large generators that make our electrical power. Look at small generators at rental places or service stations. Emphasize the safety procedures needed around electricity.

- Read some of the sections of the Ladybird Junior Science book *Levers, Pulleys and Engines* (Wills and Hepworth, 1963), which is about machines and engines. Encourage the children to experiment with some of the ideas presented.

- Rub some friction toys (toys that run by rubbing some part on a hard surface several times to set them in motion) on the floor and look for small sparks. Do the same with a carpet sweeper. Have the children ever felt a little spark or shock when touching metal after sliding their feet along the carpet? Have they noticed how clothes sometimes stick to them or each other after being in the dryer? Can they make sparks while brushing their hair? These simple examples of friction all produce static electricity.

- Experiment with waterwheel type toys in water tables or sandboxes and talk about what makes them go faster or slower. See if you can feel anything move as the wheel turns. Discuss how people used waterwheels for power (and how in some places they still do). Look for pictures of waterwheels and mills. Where would be a good place to find water for such use? What else can make things move?

◆

Windmills Turning
(to the tune of "Frere Jacques")

Windmills turning, windmills turning
Round and round, round and round
Turning wheels that work for us
Grinding grain without a fuss
Round and round, round and round.　　*(have children move arms up and down, windmill fashion)*

Windmills turning, windmills turning
Round and round, round and round
Pumping water on the farm
Making power without harm
Round and round, round and round.　　*(repeat arm motions)*

Show the children pictures of windmills. Explain that windmills have large blades on them to catch the wind. As the wind turns the blades, the force is used to turn a generator connected to the windmill. Long ago, wind was used in that way to turn wheels that milled or ground grain into flour, hence the name "windmill." Windmills are now used to pump water and drive generators for electricity. (Look up "windmills" in an encyclopedia for pictures and explanations.) Talk about what problems wind power might have.

Look for pictures of mills and talk about how grains are ground into flour. Read the story of the Little Red Hen. Visit an old farm or village type of museum, many of which have exhibits explaining this process in detail. Find out how grain mills work today. Do they still use wind or water power?

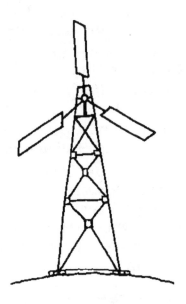

Make Pinwheels

Make pinwheels to demonstrate how wind hits blades to make them turn. You'll need an 8" x 11" piece of paper, scissors, a pushpin, and a twig or pencil with an eraser at the end.

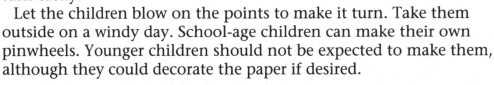

To make the pinwheel, cut the paper to form an 8-inch square. Fold the square on its diagonals so that the folds form an X. Unfold the paper and cut along the folded lines about one-half to two-thirds of the way toward the center (there will be four cuts). Take the tip of every other corner and curve it toward the center. Attach the points at the center with the pushpin. Attach the

pushpin to the twig or the eraser top of the pencil. Make sure the parts are assembled loosely so they will turn easily.

Let the children blow on the points to make it turn. Take them outside on a windy day. School-age children can make their own pinwheels. Younger children should not be expected to make them, although they could decorate the paper if desired.

The Elevator

There's a place like a box for a giant	*(stretch arms over head to form a big box)*
With doors that open and close	*(bring hands together and then pull apart)*
It feels like a moving closet	
Up and down is how it goes!	*(bend up and down)*

On its wall are some buttons with numbers
You press when you step inside.   *(pretend to press numbers)*

It waits until everyone's ready	
Then the elevator gives you a ride	*(crouch down)*
Whooosh! It goes up to the top	*(jump up)*
I wonder how it knows just where to stop?	

Things Go Up

   Ask the children about their experiences with elevators. How does it feel when they go up or down very fast? Where do they use elevators? Have they been in very tall buildings with many floors? How many floors? Think about what people did before there were elevators. You might also discuss how elevators are necessary for people in wheelchairs or with crutches.

   Experiment with pulleys from the top of a climber. Attach a bucket or basket to a rope that goes through a pulley. Allow children to raise and lower the bucket. Put some things in the bucket (blocks, animals, toys) and think about how the bucket works like an elevator.

◆

The Escalator

Have you ever seen that funny kind of stair
That comes out of the floor and goes up in the air?
You step on it and up or down you go
To the very next floor before you know.

It looks like stairs as it moves along
But when you get to the end, it's suddenly gone.
Where it goes is a mystery
Though after a few steps, another one you'll see.
Those funny stairs are really fun
But on them you must be careful and never run.

Things Go 'Round

Show the children a toy tractor with rubber treads around its wheels. Notice how the tread keeps turning around as the tractor moves. Put a sticker on the tread so you can observe how the same spot comes back on top. Think about how that might be similar to the escalator. Think about other things that might work in the same way.

◆

A Computer Story in Verse

There's another machine that looks like a TV
It's the smartest machine there ever could be.
It works with things called tapes or disks
And when you press buttons it starts writing lists.

We read what it says and press some more!
Then on its screen come words and games galore.
But that smartest machine can only do
What people somewhere have told it to.
And the way people tell it is·in a code
Called a "program" that the tape or disks hold!

Though it may seem so smart, it's really not true
For machines cannot think like people do.
People "invent" all these machines that we use,
When a machine invents a person that will really be news!

Imagination Machines

Use "A Computer Story in Verse" to talk about computers and explain things such as programming and "inventing" things. Relate the poem to computer games or electronic activities they might know. Be sure to point out that people make up and create all of these things. Talk about the many ways computers are used for work and play. List all the different uses the children tell you and keep adding to your list as you discover or think of new ones.

Encourage the children to invent pretend machines. Look at pictures of old machines and imaginary ones such as those found in Dr. Seuss books or study this picture. (Let the children invent uses for the picture.) Bring in scrap materials and bits of junk to use to create some imaginary machines. Several children could work together on a creation and think about things they might use in designing their machine. The machine may change over time as the children work on it. Hardware stores, garages, junkyards, and lumberyards may be good sources for collecting scrap materials.

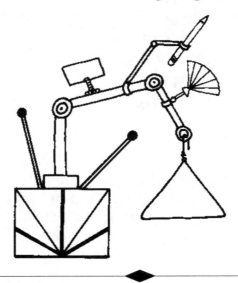

The Copy Machine

The copy machine does tricks I think
It makes us copies as quick as a wink
It takes a picture of what it can see
And prints lots of them for you and me.
In offices, people say, "Copy this quick"
And then they get mad when the copier's sick!

Making Copies

Take the children to see a photocopying machine. Take along a small doll or teddy bear and make a copy of it. You can also make copies of children's art. Explain that something like a camera inside the machine takes a picture of the object and then prints it on paper. Show the children copies of notes to parents or other things you have copied so that you had enough for everyone.

What other ways are there to make copies of something? Show the children how carbon paper works. Let them write on a top sheet and place a piece of carbon paper and a second sheet of paper under the carbon paper. What happens if the carbon paper faces the wrong way? Experiment with different ways of writing (pressing very lightly or using crayons or markers). What happens? How many copies can be made with carbon paper?

Experiment with making rubbings. Cut some letters out of sandpaper. Put a piece of paper over the letters and rub it with the side of a crayon to see what happens. Which way would be easier to make many copies of something? Can they think of reasons why people want to make copies of something?

The Typewriter

Clickety, clickety, clickety, clack
The typewriter sounds like a train on a track
Our fingers are running all over the keys   *(imitate typing)*
And letters appear on the paper with ease.
Typing machines type the words that we tell 'em
But I wonder how it knows how to spell 'em!

Office Machines

- Set up a dramatic play area using an office as a theme. Provide a typewriter, adding machine, telephone, calculator, or any other types of business machines (rummage sales sometimes have fascinating old machines for very little money). Add other office props such as paper clips, staplers, note pads, and hole punches.

- Take the children on a trip around your school, home, or a public building such as a library and look for machines. Talk about how each machine works and what each one does for people.

- Make up stories about machines. Write these stories down as you and the children create them. Have the children act out those that are suitable or have the children dramatize machines at work.

- Make lists of things people use every day at home, at school, in the office, at work, or at play. Use these lists to generate ideas for murals or books you can make up about machines such as "Machines at Home," "Machines for Kids," or "Machines for Grown-Ups." Have the children find pictures of machines in newspaper and magazine ads and collect them to use in all of these creations.

Machines Around the House

The Washing Machine *(author unknown)*

The washing machine, the washing machine
The clothes go in dirty, the clothes come out clean
The most wonderful machine you have ever seen
The washing machine, the washing machine.

The Toaster

There's a machine in our house we use every day
It cooks our bread in a special way.
We drop it in slots, four slices at most   *(hold up four fingers)*
We push down a little button   *(children crouch down)*
And soon up pops—toast!   *(children jump up)*

The Vacuum Cleaner

There's a cleaning machine that makes lots of noise
And sometimes eats up parts of my toys,
I really don't like it, not one little bit
But my mother seems very attached to it.
She loves to run it along the floor
When I hear it I run to close my door.
"Keep away from my toys," I always say,
But Mother says, "You should put them away!"

Guess Which Machine

Make up a circle game using machines as the theme. Have the children walk around in a circle as they chant "What kind of a machine do you want to be, want to be." Ask one child to choose a machine and do an action related to that machine. All the children imitate the same action while chanting, "We can be a _____machine, a _____machine, a _____machine and we _____today." Repeat the first line and ask another child. (May be chanted a few times to the tune of "Mulberry Bush" while the child thinks about a choice.) Some examples are:

MACHINE	WORK	ACTION
lawn mower	mow our lawn	pushing the mower
typewriter	type with fingers	typing a letter
telephone	call a friend	dial and talk

The Telephone

My favorite machine is a wonderful thing
It's always going, "b'ring, b'ring, b'ring"
I love to pick it up and say, "Hello"
And press all the buttons on its face, you know
You talk in one place and listen in another,
But the trouble with it is, it's always for Mother.

The Noisy Kitchen

The microwave goes "beep, beep, beep"
When its cooking job is through
The coffee pot goes "drip, drip, drip"
To make a cup for you
The dishwasher goes "swish, swish, swish"
With all those dishes to do
But the refrigerator and stove don't make a sound
Though they keep busy, too.

Mixing Machines

A blender is used to make a milkshake
And a juicer other drinks can make   *(pretend to drink)*
A mixer helps Mother make a cake   *(pretend to stir)*
Into the oven she puts it to bake   *(pretend to put in oven)*
When we eat it, we get lots of crumbs on the floor   *(pretend to eat)*
But the Dustbuster picks 'em up and a whole lot more *(make vacuuming motions)*

So many helping machines on our kitchen shelf
But I like to mix things all by myself   *(pretend to stir)*

Sorting Machines

Make a categorizing game of machines found in the home. Cut out pictures of various rooms in the house, including the garage, basement, and bathroom. Talk about what we call each room and discuss what people usually do there. Mount the pictures on small boxes (children's shoe boxes usually work well).

Cut out pictures from magazines, newspapers, and catalogs of things commonly found in homes. Include pictures of small and large appliances, hair dryers, electric razors, TVs, stereo equipment, clocks, tools, cars, bikes, toys, lamps, and yard work equipment. Mount all these pictures on file cards or heavy paper for easier and longer lasting use.

Let the children look through the file cards and sort the items in appropriate boxes according to the room in which the item would most likely be used or found. (Note that many items could be used or found in several rooms. Therefore this is not a game of right or wrong answers, but one that lets children organize things as they think about them.) The game can provide good conversation starters about things children and their families like to do as well as provide lots of opportunities for building vocabulary.

The TV

The most popular thing in our house seems to be
A thing that we watch and it's called a TV
It has a big screen where the pictures appear
And it seems like the people are really right here.

Sometimes it tells us to buy this or that
Like cereals or toys or food for the cat
Mother says it's not always true
That the toys do what they say they do
And it's hard to tell what's real or pretend
Or where some of the stories begin or end.

The TV is also where we show
A lot of my favorite videos
And sometimes play games like Nintendo
The TV has dials and buttons you use to pick a show
But how it all works, I really do not know.

Understanding TV

"The TV" introduces many concepts to talk with children about: real or pretend, commercials and selling things, changing channels and choosing shows, as well as the technical and mechanical features of a television. Certainly this is just the tip of the iceberg in questions and concerns surrounding the television, which is a powerful visiting force in most homes (and one that requires thoughtful, age-appropriate education and guidance). Activities may also be useful in helping children understand more about TV. Some suggestions follow:

- Look up "television" in a children's encyclopedia or locate "Let's Find Out" books from the library to help explain to children how the television works.

- Make a pretend TV by cutting an opening in a large appliance carton. Have the children act out a variety of actions (give a news of the day report or a weather report; do show and tell; act out a story such as "The Three Bears"; dress up and perform like singers, TV characters, or rock stars; create a commercial to sell something). Let the children think up and plan other things to do or present on TV. Talk about all the steps involved in doing something on TV and how it felt to be performing. Which things felt real or pretend to them. What did they say to try to sell something in a commercial? Was it true or did they make it up or exaggerate to make it sound good?

- Bring in puppets from "Sesame Street" or other TV related character toys. List some of the children's favorite TV shows. In discussing what the children like about these shows, ask them if they can figure out which parts are part of real life and which parts are pretend. "Mr. Rogers' Neighborhood" does a good job of illustrating this concept in the way he presents his programs. The concept of pretend is less clear in a show such as "Sesame Street," which mixes up its presentations of information and fantasy as well as mixing in cartoons, puppets, and real people.

Many other favorite children's shows do the same thing. Talk about the shows where people dress up and play parts, as opposed to the ones where toys are actually doing the acting in a cartoon format as in the Ninja Turtles. Think of all the shows that are toy cartoons. Can the toys really do the things they do on TV? Who makes up the stories or "script" for the toys? Have the children make up some stories or scripts for the TV character toys to act out. Look through library books or visit a museum exhibit on how cartoons are made to help children begin to understand this concept.

- If you have access to a video camera, make a video of the children doing their regular activities both indoors and out. Film short segments at a time when the children are unaware of your filming. Also, videotape the children doing special performances such as acting out a story, playing TV characters (perhaps some scripts they have made up), or performing musical presentations.

Show the videos to the children and talk about the different scenes. Think about what each video shows in terms of "real," "pretend," and "acting." Of course, children love to see themselves on the screen and they may be much more interested in just watching themselves without thinking about these complex subjects. Even if your discussion gets lost, the process they have participated in will not, and the four- and five-year-olds may begin to grasp some of the concepts this activity illustrates.

Show the videos to the parents; both as an example of the children's daily activities (parents love to see their children on video) and as a discussion of TV. With both parents and children, the discussion might include some guidelines for choosing shows as well as a general discussion of amount of time for and uses of games.

The Stereo

I like to listen to our stereo
It plays lots of music I know *(make swaying motions)*
I can march, or dance, or jump just so *(imitate each action)*
And with headphones I can make it music to go! *(pretend to put on headphones)*

Making Music

Show the children pictures of the different machines we use to listen to music (radio, tape deck, tape recorder, VCR, record player, compact disc player, Walkman portable stereo) or show them the real machines if you have them available. Be sure to name each one.

If you have a tape recorder, make a recording of the children singing, talking, or playing musical instruments. Ask them what music they like to listen to and think about how different kinds of music tell us different things—musical themes from familiar shows tell us what is coming, some music makes us want to dance or go to sleep. Play samples of music and have them show or tell you what the music tells them.

The Electric Toothbrush

I used to brush my teeth with a little brush
That I moved up and down all by myself *(imitate toothbrushing)*
But now my brush can wiggle and jiggle
And when it brushes my gums I sometimes giggle
It shakes my hand as it moves along
And seems to sing a toothbrushing song!

Daddy's Razor

The electric razor goes "buzz, buzz, buzz"
Daddy says he uses it to cut his "fuzz" *(imitate shaving)*
Sometimes his face may feel kind of scratchy *(feel face)*
But he runs this machine all over his face *(pretend to work razor and buzz)*
And then it feels so smooth every place *(feel face all over)*

"If I didn't shave my face most every day
I'd have a beard like Grandpa," he'd say *(pretend to rub beard)*
Only I bet you it wouldn't be gray.
When I grow up, I'll have a razor, too
And because I watch my dad, I'll know just what to do.

Let's Try Shaving

Discuss some of the ideas in "Daddy's Razor" with the children. Do they know men with beards? What color are the beards? Why do they think some beards are gray? Have they felt men's scratchy faces? Whom have they seen shaving? What different ways have they seen men shave? Have they seen anyone getting a shave at a barbershop? Put out some play shaving utensils in the housekeeping play area.

Look "razors" up in an encyclopedia. What different types of razors are there? What kinds have the children seen? Bring in pictures, if you can, of new electric razors as well as the old-fashioned kind. Talk about old-time shaving brushes that were used to lather up faces before brushless shaving cream became popular.

Mix up soapsuds into a lather. With brushes, apply the suds to plastic or rubber baby doll faces. Use plastic razors to shave the soap bubbles off the dolls. Try the same activity with shaving cream. Does it work the same way? What differences, if any, do the children notice? Write up a story about what you've learned about shaving. Encourage the children to discuss ways of shaving with their grandfathers who have much experience with this topic and can tell them about the changing technology and fashions.

Tools

I have a little hammer
That I pound nails with every day,   *(imitate pounding)*
And a monkey wrench that can turn
Things every which way.   *(move hand as if turning)*

A screwdriver and a saw are fine tools for me   *(imitate sawing)*
But my mom and dad's tools work with electricity.
They plug them into a socket to make them go.   *(pretend to plug)*
Power tools is what they're called, you know.

As they turn or cut, they whirl and hum   *(make a humming sound)*
And before you know it, the work is done.   *(clap hands)*
But we must be careful and stay away!
Power tools are not for play!   *(shake finger in a "No" gesture)*

Machine Shop

Set up an area for taking apart old machines. Collect old, nonworking machines such as clocks, telephones, radios, children's tape recorder, or sewing machine. Put these out along with some tools such as short-handled screwdrivers, small pliers or wrenches, and scissors. Encourage the children to take apart the machines carefully using the tools. Use plastic dishpans to store parts and tools.

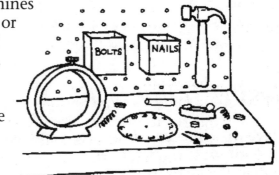

The children may enjoy reassembling the machines or using the tools or parts to play machine shop or fix-it shop. Add such things as small amounts of nuts, bolts, wire, tape, wood scraps, or pegboard, which may be useful for repairing or putting together machines.

Take a field trip to a hardware store to purchase small items for the repair shop or to look at interesting machines. The children can make signs for their shop or write up some stories or directions about the machines. Be sure to use the children's own ideas about things their repair shop needs and types of work done in the shop. They may decide to make very different things with the parts.

◆

Out and About

Buckle Up

We hop in the car to go for a ride   *(pretend to open door and climb into car)*

My brother's in the car seat by my side   *(pretend to put baby in car seat)*
I fasten my seat belt across my lap   *(pretend to put on seat belt and fasten it)*

And push it together with a loud snap
Whether we're going near or far   *(pretend to drive car)*
We must always buckle up inside the car! *(again, fasten belt)*

The Traffic Light
(to the tune of "Twinkle, Twinkle Little Star")

Twinkle, twinkle traffic light
Changing colors, shining bright
You can tell us what to do
Stop and go depend on you
When you twinkle red or green
We do exactly what you mean

Making Traffic Signs

Have the children paint some paper plates red and green. Print "Stop" on the red ones and "Go" on the green ones. Tape tongue depressors to the backs of the plates for handles. Use "The Traffic Light" for a marching game. As the children march and sing, hold up the paper plate signs at random and have the children follow the sign directions. Let children take turns being the sign handler.

The Safety Song

Red light, red light, what do you say?
I say stop and stop right away.
Yellow light, yellow light, what do you say?
I say wait and stay that way.
Green light, green light, what do you say?
I say go but look each way.
Thank you, thank you, red, yellow, green
Now I know what traffic lights mean.

Yellow Light

Paint some paper plates yellow and print "Wait" on them. Tape tongue depressors to the backs of the plates for handles. Talk about the yellow sign and what wait means. As you sing "The Safety Song," add the motions of looking each way on green. Use a fast march or run and have the children slow down when the yellow appears and get ready to stop. Talk about how cars have to slow down to stop and how the yellow light gives them warning to do that.

Pumping Gas

See the gas pumps all in a row,
Lower the hose, push the crank,   *(imitate actions)*
Put the nozzle in the tank,
Squeeze the handle,
And hear the gasoline flow.

S - s - s - s - s
Watch the pump,
Look at those numbers go!

Gasoline

Cars and trucks and trains and planes
All run on gasoline
Which burns inside their engines
To make power for each machine.
We want to have their engines burn gas efficiently
So we use our world's oil, very carefully.

Learning about Gas

"Gasoline" (along with other verses in this section) raises interesting ideas about energy sources.

- Discuss the connection between gas and oil (an encyclopedia can give you information). No doubt, the children have heard about trying to save oil, but most young children will not connect the idea that the gas we use in our cars comes from oil. Think about how the gasoline gets to the gas pump and where it is stored.

- Talk about the commercials they have seen for cars and what the commercials say about gas mileage. What does that mean? Tell them to look at the dials on their family car that keep track of mileage and the one that shows how full their gas tank is. Notice the connection between the two.

Have parents help in an experiment. Ask some parents to keep track of how far their car goes on one-fourth or one-half tank of gas and how many gallons they put in to refill the tank. Draw lines to show the number of miles and the number of gallons. Draw separate sets of lines for each car. This may help give the children some beginning ideas about the meaning of miles per gallon. Study the different graphs for several different cars to see which ones go the farthest on the least amount of gas—find the ones that are most efficient.

- Make a gas pump out of a toothpaste pump. Cover the pump with colored paper. Use a cap from a pen with a piece of shoelace attached as the hose and nozzle. Draw some numbers on the front. Use with small cars and trucks to pretend to "fill 'em up."

Bridges

Over and under all through the town
Bridges help move the cars around.
They carry cars and trucks over rivers and streams
And connect up miles of ramps and highways it seems.

Some bridges can even move up and down
To let boats underneath them move around.
People walk over bridges and some bridges have track
For the trains that keep running into town and back.

Some bridges are held up by supports from below
While others are suspended on cables, you know.
When these cables are all lit up at night
The bridges make a very beautiful sight.

When bridges get old they might even fall down
Like the famous one in London town.
So people keep checking just to make sure
That all of our bridges are safe and secure.

If they find any signs of trouble
They hurry to fix it, on the double!

Building Bridges

- Make a large mural depicting the ideas of the poem "Bridges." Draw a background of ground, hills, rivers, and highways. Make bridges out of cut paper shapes and paste them on the mural where bridges might be needed. Cut out pictures of cars, trucks, and trains and have children paste them on as well. Add other things to the mural such as buildings found in a town, boats on the river, trees, and anything else the children think of.

- Show the children pictures of different types of bridges. *The World Book Encyclopedia* has pictures of bridges and includes explanations about how they are constructed. The book includes some of the most famous bridges such as the Golden Gate Bridge in San Francisco.

- Try building bridges with blocks and experiment with how to make and support them.

- Take a field trip to look at different bridges in your community. Talk about the different types that you see and what seems to be holding them up. Think about places that need a bridge and what problems designers must solve to build those bridges.

- Read the book *London Bridge is Falling Down* by Peter Spier (Doubleday, 1967) and discuss the materials used to build bridges long ago and today. Sing the song "London Bridge Is Falling Down" and any other children's songs about bridges.

The Car Wash

The car wash machine, the car wash machine
The strangest thing I've ever seen
We drive the car in dirty and drive it out clean   *(pretend to drive car)*

A little light flashes and a door opens wide   *(move arms as if opening*
We go very slowly and drive inside   *door wide)*
Water squirts out all over the place   *(driving car motions)*
 And the brushes seem to be running into my face   *(pretend to squirt water)*
          (roll hands and move up
          to face)

They slide over the car to wash off the dirt   *(rub hands)*
I wonder if it's going to hurt.   *(cover face)*
It feels like the car is moving away
But the moving brushes make it feel that way!

The car wash machine, the car wash machine
The strangest thing I've ever seen
The car went in dirty and came out clean.

This verse describes one type of car wash. Talk about the other ways people wash their cars (at home, assembly line car washes). Wonder about how big trucks get washed. If available visit a truck wash. Look for pictures of cars and trucks being cleaned.

Washing Cars

Set up a car wash area indoors or out. Put several plastic cars in dishpans. Use plastic squirt jars filled with soapy water to wash the cars. Fill other squirt jars with clear water to rinse the cars. Use brushes after each cycle of washing or rinsing. Some possible "car wash brushes" are: vegetable brushes, small baby bottle brushes, small paint rollers, old curlers (foam or brush), a brayer, rolling pin, or used lint roller with short strips of rags tied around it. Explain how the brushes help wipe off the dirt.

If you wish to add a drying cycle, use towels or a small hand-held hair dryer. (Careful supervision is required if dryers are used.) Plastic cars can air dry with no problem, but repeated washing with no or incomplete drying will cause metal cars to rust.

An assembly line car wash for trikes can be set up outside in the summer. Use large squirt bottles or a hose with a spray attachment as the water source. Set up separate stations and workers for soaping, brushing and scrubbing, rinsing, and drying. (Do not use any electric dryers or anything electric outdoors around water play activities.) Again, with metal trikes, drying is important so have a large supply of towels available.

CHAPTER FOUR: New Places, New Faces

Introduction

New places present young children with an emotional challenge and many mixed feelings. Because of young children's limited grasp of time and the lack of control they have over detemining the change, new places can be very stressful. In addition, children often use daily routines to give their lives a sense of safety and predictability. There is the fun and excitement of a trip, but there is also uncertainty. Most children prefer their familiar surroundings and may even say that they are not going or, once they have gone, express the wish to go back home. Parents can be busy and distracted as they make plans and get ready to leave. They may not notice a child's anxiety because anticipating a vacation is generally a happy, positive time for families.

By taking the time in the child care setting to talk about, recite poems, do activities, and act out the experiences of going away or moving, teachers and caregivers help children cope better with these situations. Learning about trips other children and families have taken and the places they have gone provides children with a broader perspective and a base of useful information for their future travel experiences. I designed the verses in this section to provide that kind of information and serve as a jumping off point for discussions of the new places and faces they may encounter. Use the verses in the second section to talk about places parents go while the child remains home.

Moving, like travel, is a difficult transition for children, who will benefit by some thoughtful assistance with a change to a new place. Years ago when I was teaching nursery school in a home setting, I noticed that the children loved to pack up the doll corner things and move them to a different spot in the house. They would do this activity for several days at a time—back and forth, packing and unpacking. They moved the doll furniture, dishes and clothing more than once during the year. I soon realized that moving was an important experience in young children's lives because young families seem to move a fair amount. By moving the doll corner, the children could take charge of an experience over which they had no control in their own lives and play out the accompanying feelings.

Travel Adventures

Going on a Trip
(to the tune of "The Farmer in the Dell")

We're going to take a trip,
We're going to take a trip
Hi-ho the merry-o,
We're going to take a trip
(can substitute the name of child who is going on a trip)

We're going to (a lake).
We're going to (a lake).
Hi-ho the merry-o,
We're going to (a lake).
(fill in the blank depending on the destination: the mountains, city, sea, moon, Mexico, L.A., Grandma's)

We're going there (by car).
We're going there (by car).
Hi-ho the merry-o,
We're going there (by car).
(fill in the blank with the means of transportation child chooses: by bus, train, plane, boat, jeep, van, rocket ship)

We're going to be back soon,
We're going to be back soon.
Hi-ho the merry-o,
We're going to be back soon.

Additional verses:

We're packing up our clothes   *(or other items);*
We're going to see _____   *(people, places, or things)*
I'm taking my _____ with me   *(anything child chooses)*

For parents or grandparents taking a trip, or a parent who may be absent for a while, here is another version:

My _____ is/are taking a trip,
My _____ is/are taking a trip.
Hi-ho the merry-o,
My _____ is/are taking a trip.
(fill in the blank with Mom, Dad, Grandparents, or appropriate person)

Additional verses:

I'll miss them while they're gone;
We'll write letters while they're gone;
I'll call them on the phone;
They will be back soon.

   This remarkably flexible chant can be used in a wide variety of ways. Use it to introduce the topic of trips. It can also be used in reference to a specific child who is taking a trip, in which case that child would fill in all the blanks for her trip, talking about the specifics of the trip. Change the words to the past tense and use the verse after a child returns from a trip. The verse can also be used to think about pretend trips the group might want to take. Children can take turns picking imaginary destinations and thinking about how you get there, what you might want to take, and what you would see or do.
   The song can be used as a conversation starter about parents or grandparents who go on trips. Look up the destinations on maps and show the children where that place is in relation to where they are. Is it near or far? How can you get there? How long would it take by car? by plane? Are there bodies of water along the way? How do they cross those?
   The world of travel opens up the possibility of learning many new words associated with different places and exploring new ideas without even leaving your home base.

Let's Go

I think I'd like to go away
On this bright and shiny day!
I think I'd like to swim in the sea   *(pretend to swim)*
Or maybe, I'd like a mountain to ski   *(pretend to ski)*
I think I'd like to fly to the moon   *(squat down and jump up as if blasting off)*
But do not worry, I'll be back soon.   *(sit back down in place)*

Going Away

Sometimes it feels scary to go away
And not know where you're going to stay
It might be in a big place we call a hotel
Or a drive up version that's called a motel.

It might be a condo by the sea
Or a cabin in the woods, under a tree
It might be a house you've never seen before
Visiting aunts and uncles and cousins galore.

But your mom or dad will be there, too
To show you around this place that's new
Wherever it is, there'll be lots to do
With special people who care about you.

There will be places to go and things to see
A time for you to have fun with your family
Before you know it your trip will be done
And you'll come back and tell us about all the fun.

Chart Your Course

Discuss the ideas in "Going Away" with the children. Ask them where they have gone on trips. How many have stayed in a hotel or motel? Let them tell you about the experience. Write down their comments about the places they have been or stayed and put them together into a book or story about your group's travels. Write down the names and number of children who have been on different types of trips (visiting relatives, camping, skiing, fishing). Make a graph that represents the group's travels and shows the most popular places to visit.

Grandma	Camping	Disneyland	Lake
Keisha	Erin	Molly	Tom
Sally	Tom	Keisha	Sally
Erin	Jill		Laura
Joe	Lisa		Lisa
Molly			
Tom			
Jill			
Lisa			

The Skyscraper

Build a floor, and add a floor   *(build levels, starting low and go up, up, up)*
And another floor I see.
Do you know how many?
I bet it's fifty-three.   *(hold up five fingers on one hand; three on the other)*

Have you ever seen a building
That went up so high?   *(look way up)*
They call it a skyscraper
Can you tell me why?   *(or 'Cuz it seems to touch the sky; point to sky)*

The City

We went to visit a city
A place where the buildings are tall.
It really seems a pity
'Cuz the cars go so slow, they crawl.

There were so many roads and bridges
For the buses, cars, and trains.
And a funny thing I noticed
The streets had numbers for names.
There was a park with a zoo in the middle
And enormous places for games.

My mother said the tall buildings
Were really people's homes
And the covers on the stadiums
Were something they call domes.

We went to places called museums
With millions of interesting things.
But the art ones were just full of "see 'ums"
And a lot of pictures of kings.

If you ever visit a city
I hope you can see it at night.
It really looks so pretty
'Cuz its buildings are covered with light.

Travel Books

Let the children make books about a variety of trips based on their own experiences or the ideas suggested by poems and your discussions. Collect pictures from magazines, travel brochures (travel agents are good sources), and sporting goods catalogs of people traveling and sightseeing. Print the text dictated by the children on each page of the book and let them paste appropriate pictures from your collection to illustrate their homemade books.

A Camping We Will Go
(to the tune of "The Farmer in the Dell")

A camping we will go, a camping we will go
We'll load the car and travel far, a camping we will go

A camping we will go, a camping we will go
We'll find a site to spend the night, a camping we will go

Additional verses (add motions where appropriate): We'll cook outdoors and make s'mores; A tent might be our home you see; We'll count the stars and look for Mars; Into the woods with all our goods; We'll wash in the lake and dry with a shake; We might hear the sound of animals around.

Let's Go Camping

Set up a pretend campsite in your dramatic play area or outdoors in your play yard. If you have access to a play tent, set that up in the area or use a large sheet or lightweight blanket draped over a table or climber. A small play pool can serve as a pretend lake.

Assemble some items in a camping prop box to use in your campsite play areas. Items to include: flashlights, boots, knapsacks, lanterns, fishing poles (made out of small poles with string and magnets attached), paper or plastic fish with paper clips on them, some old pots, a few books with pictures of fish, small animals or birds, catalogs of camping equipment, packages from dried food or food containers. Add sleeping bags or backpacks to use as needed.

Trail Mix Recipe *(for a snack to eat while camping)*

Equal amounts of chopped peanuts, sunflower seeds, chopped dried apricots, chopped pumpkin seeds, and raisins. Mix all ingredients together in a large bowl and eat. If you wish, add coconut chips or other dried fruit.

At the Beach

Listen to the waves as they splash on shore.
They keep on coming more and more   *(imitate wave action)*
I start to jump as each wave rolls by   *(jump)*
But sometimes it splashes me up to my thigh. *(pat thighs)*
I watch the motorboats whizzing by
Dig in the sand and pile it high   *(make imaginary sand castles)*
At the beach the time just seems to fly!

   Ask the children if they have seen waves in the water. What are some of the things that make waves in water? Why are there larger waves in oceans? Have any of the children been in a motorboat? What does it feel like when the boat goes over waves? Be sure to discuss the importance of wearing a life jacket in boats and being careful near water. Discuss water safety rules and write them down. Talk about the rules and review them if children are going on trips to the seashore.

The Perfect Place

A pretty spot with rocks and trees
Where we can feel the gentle breeze   *(tilt head back as if feeling the breeze)*
Water rippling along the shore   *(move arms, wrists, and hands)*
As we watch the seagulls swoop and soar *(swoop arms down and up)*
I dig my toes into the sand   *(wiggle feet)*
And inside I feel just grand.   *(end with a big smile)*

Make Seascapes

Use blue paint to fingerpaint and make wave-like motions with fingers. The blue finger paint papers make nice backgrounds for seascape collages. Use stickers or cut out pictures of boats, fish, and shells to decorate the seascapes. Plastic bubble packing material makes an interesting effect when small pieces of it are glued on—like bubbles in the water. Fish shapes cut out of bright colored wrapping paper look pretty swimming in the water.

About Sailboats

See the sailboats gliding by
Their sails make triangles against the sky
They bounce along through wind and wave
I bet the sailors are very brave!

The Sailboat

A sailboat has a very tall mast   *(hold arm up high)*
That holds its sail in place   *(raise arms over head to form a triangle)*
When the wind blows, the boat goes fast *(pretend to blow and move arms fast)*
And I feel the wind on my face   *(rub face)*

Small Boats

- Make small boats by using bottle caps stuffed with florist clay, small amounts of playdough, or small pieces of Styrofoam for the base. Use small triangles cut from construction paper for the sails and toothpicks for the masts.

You can also make sailboats by using small bars of Ivory soap or corks as their base. Experiment with several different "models" of sailboats in a dishpan or small pool to see which ones sail the best.

- Make larger sailboats from plastic detergent bottles. You'll also need scissors, bleach bottles, and wooden dowels or skewers.

Poke a hole on one side of the bottle and cut a half moon slit at the end of the same side and fold up. Be sure the bottle cap is in the closed position and screwed on tight (can even be glued shut). Cut a triangle shape from a bleach bottle for the sail. A variety of colors look pretty when sailing and help children identify their own boat. Poke some holes along the longer edge of the sail and thread the wooden dowel or skewer through the holes. Place the dowel into the hole in the dish detergent bottle.

- Look up "sailboats" in a reference book and look at the types and shapes of the sails. Show them to the children and discuss what makes the sailboats go. If you wish, make some other shaped sails to use with your boats and experiment with them to see how they sail.

- Sailboats have different names based on the type, number, and style of their sails. The sails also have different names, including main, jib, and spinnaker. Explain the other words that are part of the sailboat such as the mast, which holds the sail, and the hull, which is the base of the boat.

A Sailboat Salad

Wash a lettuce leaf and lay it on a plate. Place half of a peach or pear on the lettuce with the round side of the peach or pear down. Cut a small piece of white cheese so that it looks like a sail. Stick a toothpick through the cheese to make a mast. Then stick the toothpick into the peach. Add cottage cheese around the peach.

Pebbles

I like to toss pebbles into the lake	*(imitate tossing)*
And watch the ripples that they make.	*(twirl hands)*
The little ones fall so quietly.	
But the big ones go splash!	*(clap hands on splash!)*
Down to the bottom of the sea	

Down by the Seashore
(to the tune of "Down by the Station")

Down by the seashore, early in the morning	
See the little children, ready for some fun	
See the happy grown-ups, spreading out the blankets	*(can substitute "parents")*
Watch the little children, to the lake they run	
Splashing in the water, digging in the sand	*(imitate motions)*
Splash, splash, dig, dig, the seashore is such fun!	

Sandscape Collage

Go on a shell or pebble hunt. Find shells and pebbles buried in the sand. This can be done at the beach or in a sandbox. Have each child find five or more shells and collect them in a paper cup. (If you have buried the shells yourself in a sandbox, limit the number each child finds so there are enough shells for all the children.) Have the children glue the shells on a piece of cardboard, heavy paper plate, or grocery store tray (small shells and pebbles are easier to attach than large ones). Coat the entire surface with glue and sprinkle sand over it. After a few seconds, shake off the excess sand.

The Credit Card

A credit card is small and hard   *(form small rectangle with thumb and index fingers)*

With letters and numbers on its face
But no matter what the color of the card
It works like magic anyplace
The thing about this card that is really funny
Is that it seems to work just like money!

They put it on a special tray
And on top of it some papers lay   *(imitate actions)*
A small machine slides on its track   *(slide hand across and back)*
And prints the numbers on its back
And then they write a thing or two   *(pretend to write)*
And give the papers back to you.   *(pretend to tear apart and return)*

All about Credit Cards

Discuss some of the ideas in "The Credit Card" and ask the children what they know about them. Write down their responses. Ask them if they know what it means to charge something. Where is the money that will be needed to pay for the things people charge? How will the store get its money? Ask them all the different ways people pay for things they buy. List the different places they have seen people use credit cards. What are some of the good reasons for using a credit card? Can they think of any problems that can happen with credit cards?

The Souvenir Shop

Sometimes when we go on trips we buy souvenirs
To help us remember how that place appears.
It may be a T-shirt with names of places we've been
Or pictures of special things we've seen.
The shops that we look at are full of neat stuff
But Mom says a few things to buy will be enough!

Charge It

Help the children set up a souvenir shop and a separate bank in two dramatic play areas. Let the children figure out a system for putting play money in the bank and having the bank give them some pretend credit cards to use in the shop.

Encourage the children to make or bring items to put in their gift shop. Talk about what would be good mementos for your group such as books about things at child care; pictures children have made or snapshots of people, places, and things; scrap wood projects; decorated rocks; shells; or small craft projects. Stocking and organizing the souvenir shop can become quite an extended project before it is even ready for customers. The shopkeepers will have to figure out how people can pay for the things and how they will keep track of what people "charge" and if they are going to accept credit cards. How will the bank know how much they owe the shop and whose play money account owes that money?

Let the children figure some of these things out, guiding them by the questions you raise. Remember that if the children bring things from home to use in the souvenir shop, they should be unbreakable and able to be used in play. Anything precious or fragile should be used for display only.

When Someone Else Goes Away

Mommy Went Away

My mommy had to go away
To the hospital this very day!
But she'll be back in a day or two
With a little baby that's brand new.

Four Little Babies

Four little babies in the nursery I see,
The nurse gives one to a mommy
And now there are three.

(hold up four fingers)

(hold up three fingers)

Three little babies crying boo, hoo,
The nurse picks up one
And now there are two.

(hold up three fingers)

(hold up two fingers)

Two little babies cooing for fun,
Along comes a daddy
And now there is one.

(hold up two fingers)

(hold up one finger)

One little baby is all that I can see,
But that is the one for my family.

(hold up one finger)
(pretend to rock baby)

Tell Me about It

Save these verses for the appropriate occasion, which happens with some frequency in the life of a group of young children. Insert the child's name at the beginning. Of course, discussion of new babies coming home and others who have gone to the hospital is apt to follow. Write down some of the comments the children make and create a book about new babies or going to the hospital. Keep the book to read over again while a child's mother is away and then share with her on her return. Plans might be made for the new baby to visit the group sometime in the future.

Someone's Going Away *(for extended separations)*

My _____ took a trip today   *(insert Daddy, Mommy, or*
                                              appropriate person)

To work in a place that's far away,
He/she took some clothes and our pictures, too
We hugged and kissed and said, "We'll miss you!"

I'll keep a special book while he's/she's away
And write down things I'd like to say
Then when he/she comes back in a _____ or so   *(add number of months or*
                                                  whatever time lapse is
                                                  expected)

I'll remember what I want him/her to know.

Scrapbooks

Be sure to talk about the sad feelings that are part of any separation. Help the child plan and start to keep a diary, log, or scrapbook for the parent who is away. Include pictures of the child, drawings or work the child does, and things the child wants to write in it. Make entries on a regular basis (weekly or monthly depending on the length of the separation) or as the child requests. Share this idea with the child's parent or caregiver who may want to make a similar book at home.

◆

Moving

Five Big Boxes

Five big boxes sitting on the floor   *(hold up five fingers)*
The man picks up one, and now there are four.   *(hold up four fingers)*
Four big boxes that I can see
There goes another one, and now there are three.   *(hold up three fingers)*
Three big boxes waiting by the door
The helper takes one, leaving only two more.   *(hold up two fingers)*
Two big boxes, hiding behind them is fun
The man carries one away and now there is one.   *(hold up one finger)*
One big box is taken away
Now no more are left to move today!   *(fold hands)*

The Three Boxes

A little box	*(use hands to make a small rectangle shape)*
A medium size box	*(make a slightly bigger box with hands)*
And a great big box I see	*(make a larger box with hands)*
Shall we count them?	
Are you ready?	
One, two, three!	*(repeat the motion of each shape as you count)*

Boxes to Go

"Five Big Boxes" and "The Three Boxes" can also be used as flannelboard activities. For "Five Big Boxes," use the pattern to make five large boxes from construction paper or poster board or felt. Glue small pieces of felt or Velcro fasteners to the back of the paper or tagboard boxes so they will adhere to a flannelboard. Place the five boxes on the board. As you repeat the verse, have children remove them, one at a time as directed. For "The Three Boxes," make one box of each size. In this verse, have a child put the appropriate size box on the board as you say the verse.

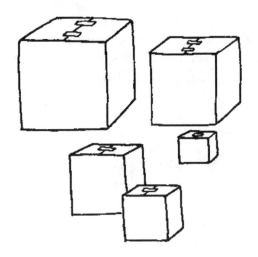

Where Do We Put It?

Collect pictures of household items (such as dishes, furniture, pots, linens, toys, clothes, and sports equipment) and organize them as if for moving. Decide where to pack each type of item. The pictures can also be sorted on a "closet" bulletin board or in small boxes for each category.

Moving Day
(to the tune of "London Bridge Is Falling Down")

Moving day will soon be here
Soon be here, soon be here
Moving day will soon be here
My dear children   *(or fill in the name of the child who is moving)*

The moving van will come along
Come along, come along
The moving van will come along
My dear children

We'll load our things into the van
Into the van, into the van
We'll load our things into the van
My dear children.

I'll take my teddy bear with me   *(let child choose special thing to take)*
Bear with me, bear with me
I'll take my teddy bear with me
My dear children.

Fill the Van

An additional flannelboard activity can be made using the box patterns and the moving van pattern. Make a large moving van out of felt. Make a number of boxes in different sizes and colors out of paper or felt.

Direct children to put a specific box in the van. (For younger children, a small box or a red box; for older children, use two conditions: a large blue box.) Count how many boxes the van can hold. Let the children experiment with ways to get the most number of boxes into the van, or the most large or small boxes into the van. Count how many of each size box in different combinations they can fit into the van.

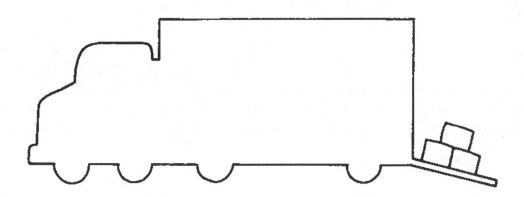

On the Move

Plan a moving day for the doll area. Let the children pack things up in small suitcases or boxes and move them to a different spot. They can move the doll corner furniture as well and set the whole area up again in the new location. Children may decide to move it back again and move again another day.

Here Come the Movers

Here comes the moving man	
He's climbing out of his great big van	(*pretend to climb out*)
He and his helpers come up to our door	(*knock on door*)
He looks at the things all over our floor	(*look around*)
Then he says to his helpers, "Okay, take this away."	(*pretend to carry a big box*)
Moving all of this stuff will take all day!	
I watch from my window as they start to load	(*look out*)
I wonder how much that van can hold.	
The men who are working seem quite jolly	
As they carry big loads on this thing called a "dolly."	(*push dolly*)
It's a funny kind of cart that has two wheels	
I wonder how heavy that big load feels?	(*pretend to hold heavy load*)

Ask the children if any of them have moved. Did their family load their things into a truck or station wagon? Or did a big moving van come to move their things from their old home to their new one? Talk about the process of moving and how hard it is to pack and carry everything. Talk about the strange feeling of leaving a familiar place and moving to a new and different one. Explain some of the words that are part of moving, including dolly, van, barrels, and cartons. Talk about ideas such as a new address, a garage or moving sale, empty walls and rooms, smaller and bigger houses or apartments, old and new neighborhoods, far away or near, missing friends, and making new friends.

Old House, New House

Make an Old House, New House chart for the children who may be moving or who have just moved. Use a picture from each setting, if you can get one, and let the child tell you things to write down on each chart. It may take a little prompting to help children think about the features of each home such as number and types of rooms, upstairs or downstairs, fireplace, porches, kinds of windows, yard, deck, garage, building materials, and roof.

Packing
(to the tune of "Paw, Paw Patch")

Wrapping up the dishes, put 'em in the barrels
Wrapping up the dishes, put 'em in the barrels
Wrapping up the dishes, put 'em in the barrels
We're packing up for moving day.

Folding up the towels and put 'em in the boxes
Folding up the towels and put 'em in the boxes
Folding up the towels and put 'em in the boxes
We're packing up for moving day

Taking all the pictures off the walls
Taking all the pictures off the walls
Taking all the pictures off the walls
We're packing up for moving day

Packing up the toys and put 'em in the boxes
Packing up the toys and put 'em in the boxes
Packing up the toys and put 'em in the boxes
We're packing up for moving day

Imitate all the motions of packing each thing. Add other items the children think of to pack.

The Three Bears

Make up a story about the Three Bears moving from their house in the woods to a new one in town. Pretend to pack up the three bowls and the three chairs. Take apart the three beds. Load everything into a big truck and drive to the city. Have the bears say good-bye to Goldilocks. This can be done as a puppet show or a flannelboard story or one they can act out. Cut up an old copy of the storybook to make puppet figures or flannelboard figures. (Use the pattern for the truck and boxes found in this chapter for additional props.) Let the children add their own ideas to the story.

CHAPTER FIVE: A Few of My Favorite Things

Introduction

Ask children what their favorite toy is and you'll get a variety of answers—from a stuffed animal to an action figure to a cuddly teddy bear. Ask them about their favorite thing to do and the answers will be equally as varied—from playing in the park to baking cookies to throwing snowballs. In writing this chapter, I picked general categories children could relate to and provided verses that would stimulate them to talk about their favorites.

The subjects presented here are varied (toys, sports, favorite verses, senses, pets, and food) but each is meant to draw children out on a specific topic. As you sing the songs and do the finger plays, you will learn more about what your children like, dislike, and know about each area. As you discuss the topics, you will learn what experiences they have had and what feelings they have encountered. By starting out with familiar topics, the children will expand them and contribute more of their own ideas and experiences.

Most of the verses in this chapter are shorter than the ones in other chapters because they describe familiar things and therefore don't need to offer as much new information. Include expanded, detailed information about the children's favorites in follow-up stories you write with them.

In this chapter, you will be the one who becomes informed as your children tell you about their specific interests. I hope you will go beyond the specific topics listed here and find out about your children's favorite things. These ideas are just for starters.

Toys and Play

My Little Train

Here comes the engine
Pulling cars along the track
Now it's going forward   *(pretend to push train forward)*
Now it's going back   *(pretend to push train back)*
Push it through the tunnel
Lift up the crossing post
I like playing with my train the most!

Teddy Bear

I have a favorite teddy bear
I take him with me everywhere
He helps me when I'm feeling sad
And understands when I'm so mad.

He stays on the shelf when I'm busy at play
And we curl up together at the end of the day
He's the greatest bear there ever could be
And when I hug him, he always hugs me.

I Like Best

Both "My Little Train" and "Teddy Bear" would serve as good introductions to the topic of favorite toys. Little trains (especially of the Brio variety) and teddy bears are popular with the preschool set so it is a safe bet some children would mention them if you asked them to name their favorite toys. Encourage the children to tell you about their own favorite toys and the things they do with them. What's their favorite building toy? What's their favorite car or truck? Do these vehicles have little people that fit inside? What dolls, stuffed animals, puppets, or cartoon action figures do they play with? What games do they make up with those items?

Ask each child to make a "My Favorite Things to Play With" book. Include pictures and dictated descriptions of their choices. Try not to limit this book to just toys; some favorite things may be computer activities, electronic games, sports, books, or art materials. Perhaps through this discussion of what children like to do we can help children think about what makes a particular toy or game a favorite—what is it that they like about something?

The Sick Dolly *(adapted fom Traditional)*

My favorite dolly was feeling sick	*(feel head for fever)*
So I called the doctor, "Please come quick"	*(dial phone and talk)*
The doctor came and knocked at the door	*(pretend to knock)*
And she looked at my dolly lying on the floor	
She looked her over and shook her head	*(pretend to examine doll)*
And told me to put her right to bed	*(carefully put in bed)*

The Silly Teddy Bear *(Traditional)*

Silly little Teddy bear
Stood up in a rocking chair   *(make rocking movements)*
Now he has to stay in bed   *(lay head on hands)*
With a bandage round his head   *(pretend to wrap head)*
Teddy bear, please take care   *(point finger for emphasis)*

Animal and Doll Hospital

Set up a small hospital corner for sick or hurt stuffed animals and dolls. Include props such as doctor kits, toilet paper rolls to use for casts, ace bandages to wrap around hurt limbs, some bandages, white coats, surgical masks, caps and gloves, old X rays, plastic play syringes, tongue depressors, and anything else used to care for the patients. Although being sick is not a favorite thing for any young child, pretending to be a doctor and taking care of sick dolls can become a favorite activity for a child who has been sick or hospitalized. The play becomes an important way of working out unexpressed feelings or anxieties about the experience. Discussing sickness, accidents, operations, or procedures; reading or writing books on this topic; and dramatic play all help the child cope with these experiences in the real world.

The Big Toy Store

I went to the toy store and what did I see?
Shelves and shelves full of toys staring at me
Boxes of games and toys from ceiling to floor
Dolls and bikes and cars and trucks galore.

So many electronic toys and games
I can't remember all their names
I had fun pretending to drive some great cars
And playing some computer games about stars.

But I couldn't decide what I liked best
So I left them all there with the rest
I'll come back another day
And try to find something "good to play."

The Little Toy Store

There's a little toy store in our neighborhood
With lots of toys that are really good,
But the wonderful thing about this place
Is all the things are out in a special play space.

There's a whole wooden Brio train set up for play
A climber and fast track and more on display
I have the best time in that little store
And always want to go back to play more.

I Want It!

"The Big Toy Store" and "The Little Toy Store" offer a chance to ask the children's opinions on what makes a toy "good for play." It also lets children talk about toy stores they have visited. Have they visited stores that match either of the above descriptions? Maybe they will even offer names for the stores. Talk about their feelings in each of these places. Do they describe feelings that fit the word "overwhelmed"? If so, help them learn the word for that feeling and talk about how that kind of place can be confusing; making it hard to know what to choose. Suggest, as the poem does, that it might be better to first think about what would be a fun thing to choose to avoid feelings of wanting everything in sight and taking the first thing you see. Parents, no doubt, will appreciate any assistance in helping children become more thoughtful and careful consumers. If there are toy libraries in your communities, talk about those as places to try out toys.

On the Shelf

Create a child-made, toy store bulletin board. Pin up strips of colored paper across the bulletin board to create shelves. Provide toy or advertising catalogs and let the children tear out or cut out pictures of different toys. Have them pin the pictures on the shelves organized by category as in a toy store. Put labels on the different groupings of toys. Children can add prices if they like for an added dimension in your discussions. This bulletin board makes a nice background for a play toy shop.

The Kite

I love to run and fly my kite   *(pretend to run and fly kite)*
It goes up to an enormous height
It whips around and goes up and down   *(move arm up and down and around)*
Oops, it's fallen to the ground.   *(lower arm and look down)*

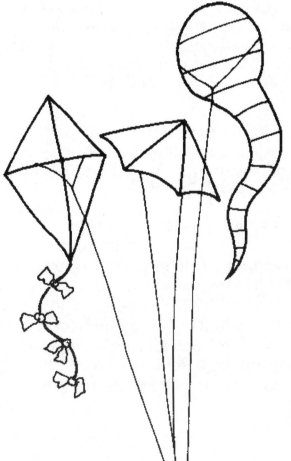

The Flying Kite *(author unknown)*

On a windy day I wish that I
Could be a kite flying in the sky.
I would climb up high toward the sun
And chase the clouds. Oh, what fun!
Which ever way the wind chanced to blow
Is the way that I would go.
I'd fly up, up, up. I'd fly down, down, down.
Then I'd spin round and round and round.
'Til I'd finally float softly to the ground.

Five Little Kites *(author unknown)*

Five little kites flying up in the sky.	*(hold up five fingers)*
Said "Hi" to the clouds as they passed by.	*(wiggle one finger for each line)*
Said "Hi" to the sun,	
Said "Hi" to the birds,	
Said "Hi" to the airplane,	
Oh, what fun!	
Then swish went the wind	*(blow)*
And they all took a dive	*(drop hand)*
1, 2, 3, 4, 5.	

Bread Wrapper Kite

A bread wrapper kite is easy to make and fly outside. You'll need two empty plastic bread wrappers, scissors, stapler or tape, hole punch, four pieces of string each about 6 inches long, and some long kite string,

For the tail, cut three 2 1/2 inch wide strips from one plastic bread wrapper. Tie the ends together so they make one long strip. Staple or tape the tail to the closed end of the other wrapper. At the open end about 2 inches from the bag's opening, punch four holes about the same distance apart. Tie one end of each piece of string to one of the four holes in the bag. Gather the four strings together and tie them to the rest of your kite string. Hold the wrapper open so the wind can blow into it. Then run into the wind. Watch the kite dip and dive.

Playing Sports

Playing sports is so much fun	
You use your body and run, run, run	*(run in place)*
Throwing, catching, kicking, too	*(imitate actions)*
Practicing sports is fun to do.	*(run in place)*
Playing baseball is so much fun	
You hit the ball and away you run	*(pretend to bat and run in place)*
Round the bases one by one	
Touch home plate to score a run.	*(tap with foot)*

Playing basketball is so much fun
You bounce the ball as you run

(run in place and pretend to bounce ball)

Down the court, dribbling is what you do
And toss it through the loop to score two.

(pretend to shoot basket)

Playing soccer is so much fun
You kick the ball as you run

(make kicking motions while running in place)

Kick with feet and knees some more
To the goal to make a score.

Play, Play, Play

Sports in preschool should be a low-key and loosely organized activity. Some children with older siblings involved in organized sports may have an idea of the object of sports, but for preschoolers provide as many opportunities as possible to play without any competitive structures. The emphasis should be on practice of the four fundamental sports skills—running, throwing, catching, and kicking—just for fun.

If the children organize some relay systems with balls or other objects that is fine, but the adult role should be to provide balls and time outdoors to use them and designate areas that can be used for running and throwing. Equipment such as fat bats, Nerf foam toys, whiffle balls, child-sized basketball hoops, paddles, small rackets, and tennis balls are useful additions for outdoor play.

The poem "Playing Sports" describes the structure of a few sports and is fine for talking about how these games are played, but the actual activity should follow the emphasis of the first verse. Children who have practice in fundamental sports skills benefit from that practice and achieve greater success later on. It is also true that the children with less natural aptitude for sports probably benefit the most from unstructured practice using these motor skills. Encourage lots of climbing, running, jumping, as well as using arms in throwing; these are all important skills to develop during preschool years.

A Sports Mural

Ask the children what sports they like best. In our professional sports oriented society, even young children are sometimes caught up in the fan frenzy. Talk about the language of various sports—the names of equipment, the parts of the playing field, the names of the player positions, and what players in that position do. Make a sports mural using pictures from sports catalogs. Organize the mural by sport and let the children paste pictures or draw some that are part of that sport. Add any comments the children make about each section. They may even know some famous players who they can draw into their mural and dictate a description such as "Michael Jordan shooting a basket." Sticker sets of sports equipment and team symbols are available, which children might add to the mural.

What Sport Is It?
(to the tune of "Row, Row, Row Your Boat")

Hit, hit, hit, the ball
Run to the next base
Hit, hit, hit the ball
Run across home base
(baseball)

Hit, hit, hit the ball
Knock it to the hole
Hit, hit, hit, the ball
Putt it into the hole
(golf)

Pass, pass, pass the ball
Throw it down the field
Run, run, to the end
A touchdown it will yield
(football)

Hit, hit, hit the puck
Glide across the ice
Slip the puck into the goal
A score would be so nice
(hockey)

Dribble, dribble, dribble the ball
Dribble to the hoop
Toss, toss, toss the ball
Throw it through the loop
(basketball)

Vary the verses according to the sport. After each verse, talk about which sport you are describing.

Talking Sports

Ask the children if they have been to see any of the games described in "What Sport Is It?" Have they watched them on TV? Talk about the names used to refer to the playing fields for these sports as well as the names of the equipment used in each sport. Talk a little (in age-appropriate ways) about how the game is played and how points are scored. This will be especially helpful for children whose families may watch sports, but haven't explained them at a child's level.

Pretending *(author unknown)*

I'd like to be a jumping jack	*(crouch down)*
And jump out from a box!	*(jump up)*
I'd like to be a rocking horse	*(hands on hips)*
And rock and rock and rock.	*(rock to and fro)*
I'd like to be a spinning top	
And twirl around and round.	*(turn)*
I'd like to be a rubber ball	
And bounce way up and down.	*(bounce)*
I'd like to be a big fast train	
Whose wheels fly round and round.	*(hands go round)*
I'd like to be a pony small	
And trot along the ground.	*(trot in place)*
I'd like to be so many things	
A growly scowly bear.	*(make growling noises)*
But really I'm a little child	
Who sits upon a chair.	*(sit down)*

The Jointed Doll *(author unknown)*

I can be a jointed doll	
Bending forward	*(bend at waist)*
Standing tall!	*(move back up straight)*
If you hold me I can walk	*(pretend to hold hands and walk)*
If you tip me I can talk	*(bend forward)*
Mama—Ma, Ma!	*(say this line as you bend forward)*

I'd Like to Be

I'd like to be a bunny	
And hop and hop all day.	*(hop)*
I'd like to be a little pup	
And run and run and play.	*(run)*
I'd like to be a birdie	
And fly and fly so high.	*(imitate flying)*
I'd like to be a buzzy bee	
And buzz and swoop and fly.	*(make a buzzing sound and swoop hands)*
I'd like to be so many things	
That I see out my door.	*(look outside)*
But really I'm a child	
Who sits down on the floor.	*(sit down)*

Let's Pretend

Talk about pretending with the children. What pretend games do they play? Ask them about some of the pretending games, especially the super hero games, you have watched them play. Write up their description of these activities the next time they get involved in pretend play. Writing about it may help them get new or more productive ideas to try out in play.

Another form of pretend play is simple dramatizations where children act out an idea or creatively problem solve and think of solutions to pretend situations. Here are some ideas to illustrate these two types of pretend activities.

- Pretend that you are Old Mother Hubbard and you have found your cupboard bare. What could you do?

- Pretend to be seeds growing in the ground with some children watering the seeds.
- Pretend to be popcorn popping. The adult can make comments about turning the heat up higher and putting on salt or butter.
- Pretend to be a favorite animal.
- Pretend to act out a role such as a baby, grandmother, astronaut, or rock star. Let them think of other roles to act out and let the children guess what or who they are.
- Pretend to punch back clouds falling from the sky.
- Pretend to stamp your feet as loud as you can, but without making a sound.
- Pretend to be a giant or a dinosaur.
- Pretend to be a piece of bacon sizzling in a pan.

Some Favorite Verses
(Traditional Finger Plays)

This Little Froggie

This little froggie broke his toe   *(hold up thumb)*
This little froggie said, "Oh, oh, oh"   *(hold up first finger)*
This little froggie laughed and was glad   *(hold up second finger)*
This little froggie cried and was sad   *(hold up third finger)*
This little froggie so thoughtful and good   *(hold up pinkie)*
Ran for the doctor as fast as he could.   *(move pinkie away fast)*

Be sure to discuss these responses and comment on each finger's helpfulness and thoughtfulness.

The Finger Band *(adapter unknown)*
(to the tune of "Here We Go 'Round the Mulberry Bush")

The finger band is coming to town   *(hands behind back, creep to the front)*
Coming to town, coming to town
The finger band is coming to town
So early in the morning

This is the way we play the drum   *(pretend to play drum)*
Play the drum, play the drum
This is the way we play the drum
So early in the morning

The finger band is leaving town   *(creep hands behind back once again)*
Leaving town, leaving town
The finger band is leaving town
So early in the morning

    Additional verses: This is the way we blow the horn; This is the way we wave the flag.

The Anthill

Once I saw an anthill   *(make a fist)*
With no ants about;
So I said, "Dear little ants,
Won't you please come out?"

Then as if the little ants
Had heard my call
One! Two! Three! Four! Five! came out   *(bring out a finger as you count each ant)*
And that was all!

The Beehive

Here is the beehive, but where are the bees?   *(make a fist)*
Hidden away where nobody sees
Soon they come creeping out of the hive
One! Two! Three! Four! Five!   *(bring out a finger as you count each bee)*

Buzz, buzz, zzzz   *(move hand all around while buzzing)*

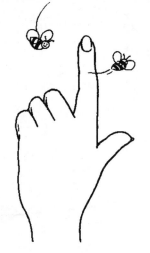

Two Little Monkeys

Two little monkeys
Jumping on the bed
One fell down
And bumped his head   *(clap hands)*
They hurried to the doctor   *(roll hands)*
And the doctor said,
"That's what you get for
Jumping on the bed"   *(point finger)*

One little monkey
Jumping on the bed
He fell down
And bumped his head   *(clap hands)*
He hurried to the doctor   *(roll hands)*
And the doctor said,
"No more monkeys
Jumping on the bed"   *(point finger)*

You can start with three, four, or five monkeys and count down repeating the verse until one little monkey.

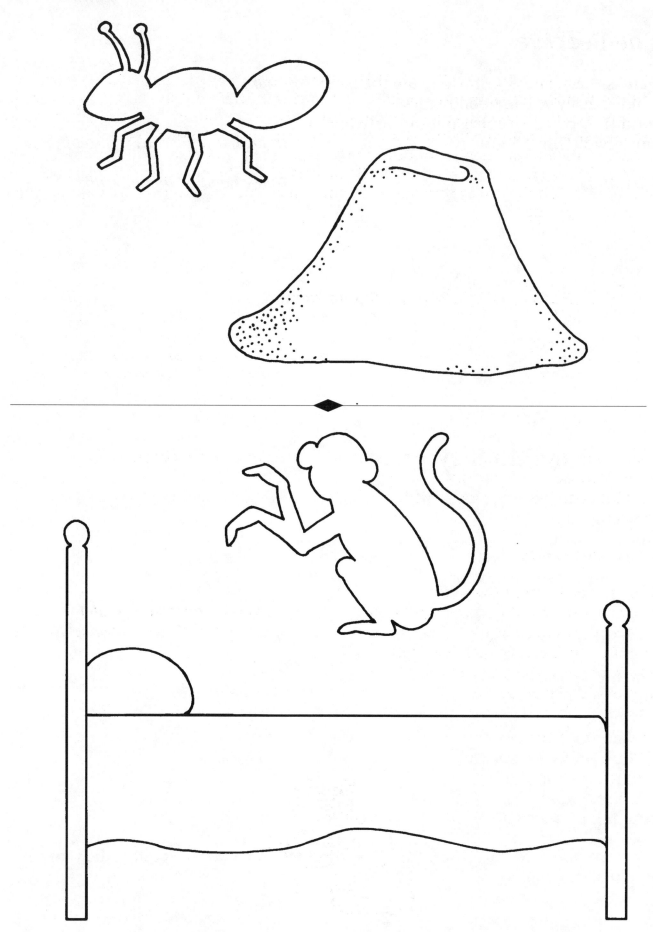

Count 'Em

You can act out "The Anthill" and "Two Little Monkeys" on a flannelboard. Use the patterns to make five ants and monkeys, and an anthill and bed. Cut the figures out of felt or use construction paper and mount small pieces of felt on the back of the figures so they will adhere to the flannelboard. For each verse, place the single object on the flannelboard (anthill, beehive, or bed). At the appropriate line, have a child or five children line up the ants or bees on the flannelboard. For the monkey verse, place all five monkeys on the bed to start and have one child come up for each verse to jump one monkey off the bed.

Roly Poly Caterpillar *(author unknown)*

Roly poly caterpillar	*(walk fingers)*
Into a corner crept	*(cover fingers with other hand)*
Spun himself a blanket	*(wiggle fingers while covering them with other hand)*
Then for a long time slept.	*(fingers still)*
Roly poly caterpillar woke up by and by	*(remove hand from fingers)*
Found himself with beautiful wings	
And all changed into a butterfly!	*(move hands as if flying away)*

Hats *(author unknown)*

When Mrs. Rabbit buys a hat	
She turns her head this way and that.	*(turn head from side to side)*
Mrs. Rabbit's hat has two	*(hold up two fingers above head)*
Holes to let her ears stick through.	
She isn't pretty, not at all	
She's only just a bunny.	*(hop around)*
She thinks her hat is beautiful	*(pretend to look in the mirror)*
But really she looks funny.	*(smile)*

Birds *(author unknown)*

If I were a bird
I would learn to fly   *(pretend to fly)*
Twisting and turning   *(move arm around)*
All over the sky
Up to the clouds, down to the ground   *(move arms up and down)*
stretching my wings, as I turned all around
Come pretend and fly with me
Back to our nest in the maple tree   *(pretend to return to nest)*

◆

My Senses

Touch *(author unknown)*

I love soft things so very much
Soft things to feel
Soft things to touch
A cushioned chair
A furry muff
A baby's cheek
A powder puff
A bedtime kiss
A gentle breeze
A puppy's ear
I love all of these.

Ask children to close their eyes and think of soft things.

How Does it Feel?

Talk about the things the children like to touch. Think of words to describe soft things such as smooth, furry, fuzzy, or fluffy. Think of things they don't like to touch and describe those things with words such as slimy, slippery, rough. Make "I Like to Touch" and "I Don't Like to Touch" charts listing the things the children suggest. You can use this same activity for other sensory experiences such as sounds, tastes, smells, and colors I like and don't like.

Sounds

I like the sound of tinkling bells
The ice cream man has come, it tells
I like the sound of crunching leaves
And wind chimes blowing in the breeze.

I don't like the sound of thunder crashing
Or sirens blaring with their red lights flashing
I don't like the screech that chalk can make
Or the hissing sound of any snake.

A Rainbow

I see a rainbow in the sky   *(look up)*
Its colors arching way up high   *(form arch with arms)*
How many colors do I see?
Red, orange, and yellow
That makes three   *(count three fingers)*
Blue and green make two more   *(hold up two fingers)*
And two shades of purple make four   *(hold up two more fingers)*

All together that makes seven   *(hold up five fingers on one hand and
                                                two fingers on the other)*

It looks like a road to heaven
But the colors fade so very fast
Rainbows never seem to last.

All about Red

Red is the color I like best
'Cuz it's brighter than all the rest
Fire engines are red and stop signs, too
And apples or tulips I pick for you
Sometimes the sky turns a fiery red
Just before the sun goes to bed.

Colors I Like

Encourage the children to make up poems about colors. The poems don't have to rhyme; they can use any words associated with that color. Is there a consensus about colors the children like and ones they don't like? What reasons do they give for liking or not liking a particular color? Do they end up liking all colors? Start talking about primary and bright colors. Later, you can add more complex colors and shades of more basic colors such as maroon, aqua, or silver.

◆

My Favorite Pet

My Puppy *(author unknown)*

My puppy is soft and furry and round,   *(pretend to pet puppy)*
He catches a bone
And he digs in the ground   *(make digging motions)*
He's taken my shoe and is running away;   *(run)*
I suppose I'll go hopping like this all day.   *(hop)*

Soft Kitty *(author unknown)*

Soft kitty, warm kitty
Little ball of fur.
Sleepy kitty, pretty kitty
Purr, purr, purr.

Have children curl up like a ball, making backs soft and round. This song is good for relaxing.

My Goldfish

My favorite little goldfish
Hasn't any toes
He swims around his little bowl
And bumps his hungry nose.
He looks at me as if to say,
"Won't you come and swim"
I wish that I could find a way
For me to play with him.

Talk about how to play with a goldfish.

Our Pets

Have the children tell you about their pets. Let them write up stories about things they do with their pets and ways they care for them. Collect pictures of pets and make up a class or group book about "Our Pets." Include the names and specific information about each pet such as what type or breed it is, what it eats, where it sleeps, its special features, age, how long the child has had this pet, and some special event or experience that happened with the pet.

◆

Foods and Cooking

Cookie Jar *(author unknown)*

I looked in the cookie jar and what did I see?
A big fat cookie Mother put there for me!
Mother looked in the cookie jar
But she did not see
That big fat cookie she put there for me!

(pretend to look)

Cooking with Children

Cooking is a wonderful activity to do with children; many cookbooks encourage child participation. The verses and activities in this chapter stress the language development aspects of cooking. When you cook, talk about what you are doing. Use the words associated with measuring and preparing, emphasize how to read a recipe and follow what it tells you. After the cooking project is complete, write up what you did in a little story, repeating all the steps in the cooking process.

My Own Cookies—Peanut Butter Dough

A first project for any age group can be making cookie dough. This recipe is easy and requires no cooking. Have the children use spoons in the mixing process to avoid the spread of germs.

You'll need a large bowl, teaspoons, mixing spoons, a jar of peanut butter, honey, powdered milk (instant or non-instant), raisins, cocoa (optional).

Start with a large jar of peanut butter. Spoon out the peanut butter into a large bowl. Add a few teaspoons of honey. Then add some powdered milk (instant or non-instant) to make a stiff dough. Mix the ingredients as you add the powdered milk. (Let the children mix after the initial start.) Add a little cocoa for a chocolate flavor. Mold the dough into shapes and decorate them with raisins.

The cookies can be eaten unbaked or you can bake the cookies in a moderate oven for 8 to 10 minutes, if desired.

◆

Mix a Pancake

Mix a pancake, stir a pancake
Pop it in the pan.
Fry the pancake, toss the pancake—
Catch it if you can!

Popcorn

Pop! Pop! Pop!   (clap hands)
Pour the corn into the pot.
Pop! Pop! Pop!   (clap hands)
Take and shake it 'til it's hot.
Pop! Pop! Pop!   (clap hands)
Lift the lid—what have we got?
Pop! Pop! Pop!   (clap hands)
POPCORN!   (say loudly)

CHAPTER SIX: Changes All Around Me

Introduction

Any attempt to help children make sense of their world must include some attention to the cycles and seasons in the natural world. Children are amazingly tuned in to nature and almost seem to notice the grass growing. They observe the natural world with a great sense of wonder; and adults, in all our busy-ness, are advised to take a lesson from children to stop and smell the roses and wonder how they got their smell.

The verses in this chapter enhance the enjoyment of the seasons' natural cycle by celebrating those cycles. They open up discussions about the cycle to increase the children's knowledge and understanding of the seasons. Of course, children begin their approach to the seasons where it affects them most—in the things they do and clothes they wear. I hope these verses and activities will help everyone appreciate and enjoy the seasons.

Seasonal Fun

All about Seasons

Summer is the season I like best
'Cuz you don't have to get so very dressed
And we have more time to play
'Cuz we seem to get a lot more day.

But fall is nice with its colorful trees
And all the fun you can have with leaves
But you need to wear more clothes when you go out
'Cuz it feels a little chilly as you run about.

Winter brings on more clothes still
I don't like snow pants or boots and I never will.
But I love how it looks on a snowy day
And snow is really fun for play.

Spring is the time that is most confusing
And I have the hardest time choosing
Which clothes to wear—one day is cold and the next one hot
And on top of that it rains a lot.

A Big Book of Seasons

Discuss with the children the ideas suggested in the poem "All about Seasons" and write down their observations of the seasons. Children are apt to have sketchy ideas about the seasons of the year because of their normal attention to the here and now and their limited memory for atmospheric conditions (young three-year-olds often don't remember what snow is when it falls again, unless they've heard much about it.)

Create a book about the seasons using photographs of the children during each of the seasons. Make sure the photographs show what they are wearing and doing outdoors. Mount those pictures on large sheets of paper according to the season. Label the paper with the name of the season and discuss how you can tell what time of the year it is. Next to the photos, write down all the things the children observe or know about that time of year. Let them add their own pictures or decorations.

Continue making large seasonal pictures as the year progresses. Put them together into a big book of seasons that you look at from time to time. The book can become a nice way of recalling things that happened over the year. Be sure these books tell about the seasons as your children are experiencing them. Don't say it snows in winter if you live in a place where it never snows. In those cases, the reference should be real experiences. (It snows at my Grandma's house in Colorado. We went to a place with snow and skied.) Include activities that may be seasonal such as football in the fall or baseball in the spring, if children mention them. Make additions to these books as the children suggest since they are apt to continually discover new things about each season.

◆

Changing Trees

Have you ever noticed that the trees
Can tell us about the seasons?
I don't know exactly why
But I'm sure they have their reasons.

In fall their leaves change color
And then fall off the tree.
But in spring new buds start growing
And soon green leaves we'll see.

Some trees grow beautiful blossoms
That in summer turn to fruit.
Trees produce different seeds
And some of them look cute.

A Tree for All Seasons

Bring in a large tree branch. Place it in a coffee can filled with sand. In the fall, make colored leaves to hang on the branches. In the winter, hang paper snowflakes or holiday items on the tree. You can hang other seasonal items, such as pumpkins, mittens, and flowering blossoms, from the tree branch as well. Be sure your choices are realistic for the season in your region.

A Seasonal Mural

Collect samples of things that are part of trees (such as seeds, pine cones, cotton fluff, leaves, and needles). Make a large mural of trees in the different seasons. Use pictures of trees or draw trunks and branches and add leaves, flowers, fruit, seeds, cotton fluff, or nuts, depending on the season. Add things like birds and bird nests in the spring and butterflies or bugs in the summer. Add squirrels and other animal life as you see it. What other things do the children think of to add to their seasonal mural? Be sure to include evergreen trees or palm trees, whichever is appropriate, in the mural and discuss how they look in each season.

Fall Favorites

Falling Leaves

This month is October
With leaves falling down   (flutter hands down)
They make a nice carpet   (move hands as if smoothing carpet)
All over the ground

Soon we will rake them   (pretend to rake leaves)
Into a heap
Then into a big pile   (take a big leap and fall down)
I can leap!

Fun with Leaves *(author unknown)*

When the leaves are on the ground	*(point to floor)*
Instead of on the trees	*(clasp hands over head)*
I like to rake a pile of them	*(raking motion)*
Way up to my knees	*(hands on knees)*
I like to run and jump in them	*(jump once)*
And kick them all around	*(kicking motion with foot)*
I like the prickly feel of them	
And the crickly, crackly sound	*(click fingernail)*

Leaf Games

Use leaf shapes of various colors and sizes for flannelboard activities, finger plays, counting activities, and games. For flannelboard use, cut leaves from felt or paste a small piece of felt on the back of a real or paper leaf. Collect real leaves and cover them with clear contact paper to use in games. Cut paper in the shape of maple, elm, oak, or poplar leaves (or others common to your area) in all different colors. Following is a list of some leaf games to try.

- Jump Up. Give each child a leaf and call out a color, shape, or both (red leaves, pointy leaves, yellow round leaves). The children with that leaf jump up. Eventually, the children may learn to distinguish the leaves by their real names.

- March Up. Give each child a leaf. Have the children find others with the same color and shape leaf.

- Counting Leaves. Call out number combinations (four red leaves and two yellow leaves) and have the children put those combinations on the flannelboard or get together in groups. Make various combinations and always count the total number.

- Shape Match. On a bulletin board, put up a picture of four different trees and an outline of the shape of the leaf that goes with each tree. Let the children pin the leaves around the tree that their leaf matches. This can also be done as an individual activity. Place the leaves in a box and have one or more children match them to the trees.

Scarecrow

Scarecrow, scarecrow, turn around   *(imitate all actions)*
Scarecrow, scarecrow, jump up and down
Scarecrow, scarecrow, arms up high
Scarecrow, scarecrow, wink one eye
Scarecrow, scarecrow, bend your knees
Scarecrow, scarecrow, flap in the breeze
Scarecrow, scarecrow, climb into bed
Scarecrow, scarecrow, rest your head

The Old Scarecrow *(author unknown)*

The old scarecrow is a funny old man
He flops in the wind as hard as he can
He flops to the right
He flops to the left
'Til he's all but out of breath.

His legs swing out
And his arms swing, too.
He nods his head in a
"How do you do"
He flippity flops when the wind blows hard
That old scarecrow in our backyard.

Fun with a Scarecrow

Make a scarecrow by stuffing bags of leaves into old clothes. Tie the pant legs at the bottom and shirt sleeves at the wrist. Place a belt around the waist to shape the scarecrow and keep its shirt tucked into its pants. By using adult-sized pants and shirts, your scarecrow will be big enough for the children to sit on as it sits in a corner or on a chair. The leaves will make a crunchy noise when squeezed or sat on. You can make smaller scarecrows for table decorations or a display in the same manner using smaller (child) sized pants and shirts and stuffing leaves in smaller bags.

Be sure to talk about what a scarecrow is used for. Ask the children if they have seen any scarecrows. Where would they most likely see one? Can they think of famous scarecrows in any stories?

Winter Favorites

It's Snowing

It's snowing, it's snowing

(make fluttering motions with hands like snowflakes falling)

Big flakes falling down
They make a white carpet
All over the ground.

(move hands as if smoothing carpet)

I like to lie down

(lie down with room to spread arms out from sides)

In the fluffy white snow
And if I move my arms just so
I can make an angel you know

(move arms up and down)

Snow Sparkles *(author unknown)*

This is a shining
Sparkling day
Everything sparkles
The prettiest way.

Everything's shiny
And everything's bright
Because of the snow stars
That fell in the night.

Stumbled and tumbled
Until they fell down
To make this a shining
And sparkling town.

Say this poem right after a fresh snow to help stimulate discussion about how the snow looks. The language in this verse is picturesque, but the children's descriptions may be even more fun, so be sure to write them down.

Wind Is Blowing
(to the tune of "Frere Jacques")

Wind is blowing, wind is blowing
All around, all around
See the snowflakes twirling
Into drifts they're swirling
Blow wind blow, blow wind blow

Snowflakes

Take dark colored construction paper outside on a snowy day. Lay the paper flat on your hands and catch snowflakes. Look at them before they melt. Talk about their designs and sizes.

Making Snow Trails

After a fresh snowfall, have several children make a trail in the snow by walking or running toward specific places on the playground (the climber, around the swing, to the largest tree). Have the other children follow each trail to see where it goes. The second group can make new trails to the other spots and the first group can follow these trails. (This activity makes a game of creating pathways to areas in a snow-covered playground!)

Winter Stories

Have the children dramatize or make up stories about:

- shoveling snow.
- pushing a snowblower (remember the sound effects).
- brushing snow off the car and scraping the windshield.
- climbing up big mounds of snow.
- building a snow fort or tunneling through the snow.
- riding on a snowmobile. Have the children sit down and pretend to be snowmobiles scooting across the floor. Don't forget that snowmobiles can get stuck in deep snow and friends have to come and pull them out
- pushing cars that are stuck in the snow.
- driving a big snowplow to clean up the streets (dumping snow in trucks and hauling it away).

Snowflakes Come Down

The snowflakes come down   *(fingers falling from above head)*
Softly calling
From my window sill;
Come out and make a snowman   *(beckoning motion; shape snowman with hands)*
And go sliding down the hill.   *(sweeping downhill motion with one hand)*

Cold Weather *(author unknown)*

Wind in the chimney, snow in the air
Frost on the window, snow everywhere
Pull on your snow pants and button your coat
Slip on your mittens and tie up your throat
Do be careful and don't freeze your noses
You'll need them next summer
To smell the roses!

Walking in the Snow

Here we go walking in the snow
Carefully stepping on tiptoe
Lift your left foot, then your right
Raise them to this tall height   *(hold hand up to shoulder level)*

Here's some ice along the side
Watch us while we slip and slide
Carefully gliding nice and slow
Then, suddenly, oops, down we go!

   Dramatize walking in deep snow and slipping and sliding on the ice. Act out this verse with children in their stocking feet—and don't forget to imitate actions.

Snowstorms

- Make up stories from the children's experiences with a snowstorm.
- Make a large mural with huge mounds painted white and cars, trucks, and plows on it. Use a John Deere or Toro catalog to find pictures of trucks, snowplows, and snowblowers.
- *Katy and the Big Snow* by Virginia Burton (Houghton Mifflin, 1943) is a good story to read after a snowstorm.

◆

Shoveling Snow
(to the tune of "Here We Go 'Round the Mulberry Bush")

This is the way we shovel the snow   *(pretend to shovel snow)*
Shovel the snow, shovel the snow
This is the way we shovel the snow
On a cold and frosty morning

What will we find down under the snow?
Down under the snow, down under the snow
What will we find down under the snow
As we shovel away this morning?

I found a boot down under the snow
Down under the snow, down under the snow,
I found a boot down under the snow
As I shoveled away this morning

   Let the children add verses of other things they might find (the driveway, the sidewalk, a mitten, a treasure). This is a good song to accompany snow shoveling or a winter outdoor treasure hunt.

The Melting Snowman
(to the tune of "I'm a Little Teapot")

I'm a little snowman, round and fat   *(make large circle with arms)*
Here is my scarf   *(wrap pretend scarf around neck)*
And here is my hat   *(hands over head to form hat)*
When the merry sunshine comes to play   *(make round circle with hands for sun)*

Just watch how fast I melt away   *(slowly fall and curl up into a small ball)*

The Snowman *(author unknown)*

The snowman fat
Put on his hat
And began to dance around.
The sun came out
Made the snowman pout
And he melted to the ground.

Spring Things

Spring

I like to see the bright blue sky
I like the air when it's warm and dry
I like to watch the budding leaves
And the beautiful, flowering trees
I like to hear the birds that sing
Everyone is happy because it is spring.

The Butterfly

Up and down the air you float
Like a little fairy boat,
I should like to sail the sky
Gliding like a butterfly   *(pretend to fly and glide like butterflies)*

Dandelions

Dandelions yellow, blooming in the grass
Pretty dandelions, I pick some as I pass   *(pretend to pick some)*
Dandelions silver, dandelions gray   *(pick some more)*
Feathery dandelions, I'll blow them all away. *(pretend to hold bunch and blow at them)*

Spring Collage Book

Ask the children to tell you all the things they like about spring. Write down their comments and continue adding to the list for several days. After you have many items on your list, group them into clusters such as the things that are related to weather (warm days, more sun and light), growing things, animal life, and playtime. Use these clusters as the themes for spring picture collages on large sheets of paper, one for each grouping. Let the children draw or cut out pictures for their collages and write a description of each collage. Put the collages and the descriptions together into a "Big Book about Spring." You can always add to it as you discover new things about spring.

The Sounds of Spring *(author unknown)*

The melting snow says, "drop, drop"
The little frog goes, hop, hop
The little bird says, "peep, peep"
The little vine grows, creep, creep
The little bee says, "hum, hum, hum"
The little flower says, "Spring has come."

Spring Is Here *(author unknown)*

Spring is here and how do I know?
Mr. Robin told me so
Spring is here and how do I know?
Robin told me so.

Spring is here and how do I know?
Pretty flowers told me so
Spring is here and how do I know?
Flowers told me so.

Have the children suggest other things that tell us spring is here, such as warm sunshine, bright green grass, baby ducklings, and growing gardens.

Six Little Ducklings *(traditional)*
(to the tune of "Bell Bottom Trousers")

Six little ducklings   *(hold up six fingers)*
I once knew
Fat ones, skinny ones   *(make wide and narrow motions with hands)*
There were, too.

(refrain)
But the funny little duck
With the feathers on his back   *(put hand on lower back and wiggle fingers)*
He ruled the others with
His quack, quack, quack   *(form quacking bill with two hands)*
Yes, he ruled the others with
His quack, quack, quack

Down to the river they would go
Wibble, wobble, wibble, wobble

(put two hands together and make wobbling motion)

To and fro
(repeat refrain)

Budding Flowers

Here's a green leaf   *(show hand)*
And here's a green leaf   *(show other hand)*
That you can see makes two.
Here's a bud   *(cup hands together)*
That makes a flower;
Watch it bloom for you   *(open cupped hands gradually)*

Plant Some Seeds

Read the story *Seeds and More Seeds* by Millicent Selsam (Harper Collins, 1959) or another book about how to plant seeds. Try some of the experiments with seeds that Selsam describes or grow your own. Write up your observations of the seeds on a weekly basis. Write down which plants are growing, when they started growing, how much they grow every few days. Draw some conclusions about what plants need to grow.

Flying Like a Bird

Up, up in the sky, the little birds fly.	*(fingers flying like birds)*
Down, down in the nest, the little birds rest	*(join hands to form nest)*
With a wing on the left, and a wing on the right,	*(put hands on hips one at a time)*
Let the little birds rest, all the long night.	*(put head to one side as if tucking under wing)*

A Home for the Birds

Five little birds without a home.	*(hold up five fingers)*
Five little trees in a row	*(raise hands high over head)*
"Come build your nest in our branches tall	*(cup hand to make nest)*
And we'll rock them to and fro."	*(rock the nest)*

If I Were a Bird

If I were a bird, I'd sing a song	
And fly around the whole day long	*(flap arms to fly)*
And when night comes, I'd go to rest	
Way up in my cozy nest	*(rest head on arms)*

For the Birds

Make a bird's nesting ball to hang on a tree in the spring. For the nesting ball, put pieces of yarn, ribbon, or string in netting cut from an onion bag. Tie and hang near a tree. Watch the birds pick at the contents. Talk about how and where the birds build their nests. See if you can find a nesting project to observe and write about.

Summer Fun

Going Fishing
(to the tune of "My Bonnie Lies Over the Ocean")

Fisher folk fish in the lakes
In rivers and streams and the sea
Fisher folk catch great big fishes
But fisher folk cannot catch me

Oh, bring back, bring back
Bring back some big fish for me, for me
Bring back, bring back
Oh, bring back some fish from the sea

Five Little Fishes

Five little fishes were swimming near the shore.	*(wiggle fingers on one hand)*
One took a dive,	
And then there were four.	*(point to thumb, then turn down)*
Four little fishes were swimming out to sea.	*(wiggle four fingers)*
One went for food,	
And then there were three.	*(point to index finger, turn down)*
Three little fishes said, "Now what shall we do?"	*(hold up three fingers)*
One swam away,	
And then there were two.	*(point to next finger, turn down)*
Two little fishes were having great fun.	*(wiggle the last two fingers)*
But one took a plunge,	
And then there was one.	*(hand in plunging motion)*
One tiny fish said, "I like the warm sun!"	*(hold up little finger)*
Away he went,	
And then there were none.	*(put hand behind back)*

Paper Bag Fish

Make some paper bag fish with a few simple materials. You'll need paper bags (small and medium), newspaper, string, markers or paints, coding dots or reinforcers, and stapler or tape.

Fold the paper bags so they lay flat. Have the children color the bags all over, on both sides, with markers or paints. Look in a book of fish to think about the colors and shapes of various fish the children might make. Use varying sizes of bags from small to medium. As each bag is finished and dry, fold the two corners of the closed end down to form a point. Staple or tape the corners to hold them in place.

Tear pieces of the newspaper into small strips and crinkle up. Stuff the bags very slightly with the crinkled newspaper. Pinch together the open end of the bag (about 2 inches from the end) and tie it with a piece of string. The end of the bag now forms the tail of the fish. Near the point, tape the coding dots or re-enforcers for eyes.

Put your fish in plastic shoe boxes to make pretend aquariums. Add marbles, shells, small plants, and other items for an under-the-sea diorama. (The children might have good ideas for these dioramas after reading the book or watching the movie *The Little Mermaid*.)

In Summertime

In summertime I play so hard
I love to run around the yard   *(run in place)*
I like to climb up all the trees   *(pretend to climb trees)*
But keep away from buzzing bees.   *(make buzz noise)*

And when the day gets very hot   *(fan self)*
Into a pool of water I plop!   *(plop down and pretend to swim)*
And then I dig in the sand for hours   *(pretend to dig)*
Making tunnels, roads, and towers   *(pack sand and pile into towers)*

Summer Mural

Make a large, summer fun mural. Spread some glue on construction paper and sprinkle sand over it for the sand areas and sand constructions. Use light blue tissue paper for water. Tie-dyed coffee filters make pretty flowers, which you can add to the mural. Cut out figures of children in summer clothes doing summer things and add to the mural. Make up a story to tell about the mural and things children like to do in the summer.

The Sprinkler

The sprinkler turns and turns around	*(have children turn)*
Spraying water all over the ground	*(extend arms out while turning)*
It waters our grass and while it's on	
I run right through it and have some fun.	*(pretend to run and get wet)*

Water Fun

Poke several holes in the bottom of plastic or paper cups and use in an outdoor water table. These new strainers are fun to use with water. Use them to add water to sandboxes that have become too dry.

Water Experiments

Fill some containers with water and experiment by putting different materials into the water. Here are some items to test:

- What happens to salt or sugar when you place a teaspoonful of each in water? (It dissolves.)
- What happens to pebbles? (They sink, but are still there.)
- What happens to corks or Styrofoam pellets? (They float.)
- What happens to pieces of cloth? (They get wet and slowly sink. Try different fabrics and plastic materials to see which absorb water and how fast they sink. Do some stay closer to the surface?)
- What happens to food coloring or paint? (It dissolves, but colors the water.)
- What happens to sand? (It sinks to the bottom.) What happens if you stir the water again?

Encourage the children to think of other things to test in the water and make up their own questions. Discuss the observations you make about water. Later, write a story about the things you and the children learned. Can you speculate about why some things sink and some float? How long does it take the different fabrics you tested to dry?

I Like Summer Book

Make an "I Like Summer" book. List all the things the children like about summer (one item per page). Illustrate each page with pictures from magazines or children's drawings.

Summer Fun

Summer brings us nice warm sun	*(make circle in air for sun)*
For swimming and fishing and lots of fun	*(pretend to swim and fish)*
For digging for rocks and shells in the sand	*(pretend to dig)*
And sunbathing to get a tan	*(stretch out arms and legs)*
How wonderful to run and play	*(run in place)*
At the beach on a sunny day.	

This Little Child *(an ode to summer bruises)*

This little child scraped her knee	*(hold up and wiggle thumb)*
This little child said, "Oh, dear me!"	*(hold up first finger)*
This little child laughed and was glad	*(hold up next finger)*
This little child cried and was sad	*(point to next finger)*
But this little child so helpful and good	*(wiggle pinkie)*
Ran for the teacher as fast as she could	*(move pinkie away fast)*

Be sure to discuss the appropriate and inappropriate ways to respond when people get hurt.

Summer Fun Ideas

- Nature Walks. Take walks to observe nature. Look for things growing in the wild, seeds that have fallen from trees (What tree do they belong to?), bugs and what they are doing, water collected in puddles or ponds and what is in them. Make books about your walks using the things collected or observed. Tell the story of how and where they found or saw the items and something interesting about each item and place. Talk with the children about taking care of things in nature and not carelessly collecting things from the outdoors. Conservation habits can be learned from an early age.

- Nature Collages. Take along some paper plates and a gummy type of glue or glue stick on your walk. As you find interesting things lying on the ground, use the glue to attach them to the plate to make a nature collage. Display the collages when you get back. Try to find out the names or kind of leaf, seed, bark, rock or other items in the collage.

Cloud Watching

I like to watch the clouds roll by
They tell a story in the sky
Some are fluffy, soft, and white
Others look as dark as night
What do the fluffy ones look like, I wonder
But the dark ones I know, bring us rain and thunder.

Clouds *(author unknown)*

What's fluffy white and floats up high	*(point upward)*
Like piles of ice cream in the sky?	*(rub stomach)*
And when the wind blows hard and strong	*(move hands sideways fast)*
What very gently floats along?	*(move hands slowly through the air)*
What brings the rain?	*(flutter fingers downward)*
What brings the snow?	*(flutter fingers downward)*
That showers down on us below	*(point to friends and self)*

Go Cloud Watching

Lie down on a blanket in your yard or in a park and watch the clouds. Repeat the verses about clouds. Talk about what things the shape of the clouds remind you of, such as animals or monsters. What makes the clouds move? What happens when the sun is behind a cloud? How can you tell where the sun is hiding? Talk about the expression "every cloud has a silver lining" and what that means. This activity is best to do on a sunny, but slightly breezy day when there are clouds in the sky.

Summer Senses

In summer I like to sniff outdoors
Just like the puppies do.   *(imitate sniffing)*
I like to smell the flowers   *(pretend to smell flowers)*
And the early morning dew
I like the smell of fresh cut grass   *(pretend to push lawn mower)*
And the taste of lemonade in a glass.   *(pretend to drink)*

Using Your Senses

   Talk about the things children smell outdoors. To explore another sense, take a walk
with a battery operated tape recorder and record sounds heard outdoors. When you
return, play the tape and identify the sounds. Categorize them into people sounds,
machine sounds, nature sounds, and animal sounds. This activity is good to do near a
lake or river. Also try listening with your "ear to the ground." Have the children put their
ears flat against the ground. An enormous amount of activity is going on under the
earth. What can they hear? What do they think is going on under the ground?

Color Mixing

   Fill some plastic squeeze bottles with water and add food coloring. Take the bottles
outside and let the children experiment with mixing colors by squirting different colors
into containers. Talk about what happens and what combinations make which colors.
What happens when they mix all the colors together? After this experiment, read the
book *Little Blue and Little Yellow* by Leo Leoni (McDowell, Obolensky, 1958).
   You may want to repeat this activity a few times to see if the children get more skilled
at controlling their color mixing. The squeeze bottles can also be used to paint with on
large pieces of brown craft paper or rolls of shelf paper taped to the sidewalk. Encourage
the children to make different design patterns by moving the bottles as they squirt.

Barefoot Painting

Tape down large sheets of craft paper or newspaper outside. Mix soap flakes into liquid tempera in aluminum pie tins. Place the tins next to the paper. Let the children step barefoot into the tempera and paint with their feet on the paper. Encourage them to tiptoe or use toes and heels as brushes. Add sand to the paint for texture.

CHAPTER SEVEN: Special People, Places and Events

Introduction

Defining relationships, celebrating holidays, and visiting places are all parts of a growing child's life. Because sometimes it is hard for children to relate to all the different aspects of their life, the preschool can help children appreciate and understand all the special people, events, and places they encounter.

Most of us may have forgotten how we tried to sort out our relatives and figure out how relatives we didn't see often were connected to us. For the young child with limited abstract reasoning skills, defining family relationships is a real puzzle. The more ways we can help put these connections together, the more we can help the children in their own families. An important message is that this extended family cares about the child. Talk about real experiences that children have with their extended families. Of course, family relationships are always evolving, but talking about them can help children develop positive ways of looking at these relationships.

All children have had the experience of being overwhelmed, frightened, or generally upset by some special event or place, which had been intended as an exciting venture. Trips to amusement parks or a big holiday parade can overstimulate children; they may not even understand what's going on. Parents may experience disappointment if special events they have been working on don't turn out to be as successful as they had hoped. Again a little education, exposure through verse, active playing out, and discussion can pave the way for more successful real experiences. A child who has been roaring like a lion during a week of pretend circus parades is not as apt to be frightened if the lion in the real circus does roar.

The poems, action verses, and activities in this chapter will help children learn more about some social experiences. They are also intended to stimulate discussion about the experiences the children have had so they can make better sense of them. Most of the discussion questions ask about things they like and are positive in their approach. I encourage you, however, to discuss with the children things they did not like or understand. Ask them what made them frightened or upset. By talking about these parts of experiences, we help children learn coping strategies. For many of us, experience is the best teacher. But without discussion, interpretation, and help from caring adults, experience may not teach what we want it to.

Special People

Grandmas

Some grandmas live near
Some grandmas live far
But grandmas love you
Wherever they are.

Grandpas, aunts, and uncles, too
Always want to know about you
These are special people for you and me
For they are part of our family.

Family Books

Let the children tell you about the special people in their life. (You may need some additional information from parents to help interpret what the children say.) Make up a booklet for each child about members of their extended family. Include where the relatives live, what the child likes to do with them, and any other special things the child mentions. *Kevin's Grandma* by Barbara Williams (E.P. Dutton, 1975) is a good book to read to start a conversation on this topic. There may not be too many grandmothers like that one, but you never know what grandmas may be up to these days.

At Grandma's House

We go to Grandma's on each special day   *(pretend to drive)*
She has a lot of special games I like to play   *(pretend to play)*
Some are old, but look quite new
Mom and Dad like to play them, too!
My cousins and I like to play outside.
We like to run around and hide   *(pretend to run and hide)*
There's always lots of good food to eat   *(pretend to eat)*
And for dessert there's a special treat.   *(ask children what it should be and pretend to eat)*

Going to Grandma and Grandpa's House

- Discuss the games the children find at their grandparent's house. Who might the games belong to? Wonder about what the house was like when their mom or dad lived there (if the grandparents still live in the same house). Do their grandparents tell them stories about when their parents were little?

- Play "I'm going to Grandma's" and think about what you could take. Have each child name something and repeat the items that the others have said. How many things can they remember?

- Take a pretend trip to a grandparent's house (like going on a safari). Get ready, pack bags, load up the car, climb into the car seat, drive, look out windows. (List things seen such as cows, barn, woods, river, and tall buildings.) Stop for gas or wait for a train until you finally arrive. Run into the house, hug and kiss grandma and grandpa. Sniff the air. What good smells do you smell? Guess what it might be.

Brothers and Sisters

Brothers and sisters are lots of fun
They play with you and chase and run   *(run in place)*
But sometimes they tease and call you names
And won't let you play some of their games   *(shake finger)*
But most of the time it's nice to be
With brothers and sisters in a family   *(make hugging gestures)*

Fighting

Sometimes I fight with my brother
It just starts when we're fooling around.
And it really bothers our mother
When we're rolling all over the ground.

She says she's afraid we'll get hurt
And sometimes it does hurt a bit
But the thing about fighting with a brother
Is that both of us kind of like it.

All about Brothers and Sisters

Siblings are indeed special people to each other as they live through the early stages of what may be their most long-lived and enduring relationship. Of course in later years in our mobile society, siblings often live far apart. But during the early years, their lives are completely connected and intertwined so talking about this subject is important. Let the children tell you what fun things they like to do with their siblings. What troubles do they have with siblings?

Make charts of the things the children like and don't like about their siblings. You might want to design separate charts for sisters and brothers to see if there are different responses. From all the specific things children tell you, come up with some generalizations about these relationships to put in a big book about brothers and sisters.

Research tells us that what people most remember about their siblings is that they had fun together. Do your findings agree? What fun things do the children do with siblings? Do they fight? How do they feel about it? For those who have baby siblings, you might make a pro and con chart. Share these charts and books with parents at a meeting or get-together. Most parents only get to see their own inner family circle and may be concerned about their children's interactions at home. Learning something about how the children view this and how other sibling pairs interact could be enlightening to all.

Follow up this beginning discussion by expanding ideas about siblings. Make lists or charts on such topics as nice things I did for my brother or sister; something nice my brother or sister did for me; something I wish my brother or sister would do; things I share with my brother or sister.

My Wish

If I could have an
Only wish
Now wouldn't that
Be fine
I'd wish that
Everybody had
A mother just like
Mine.

Mother

Who ran to help me
When I fell
And had some funny
Story to tell
Or kissed the place to make it well?
My mother.

Gifts for Mom and Dad

Hand plaques made from plaster of Paris have been a great favorite gift for parents on their special day, but you can also make handprints and footprints on paper, tagboard, cloth type wallpapers, paper plates, grocery store storage trays, place mats, or shoe box lids. Handprints made on these materials won't break and are the most long lasting. Mount the prints on another paper or decorate them (glue on rickrack, yarn, glitter, stickers, lace trim, little flowers, or pieces of ribbon. Attach a yarn loop or rubber band suspended from the top so that the parents can hang the print. "Here Are My Hands" is a favorite verse to accompany handprints or footprints (see below).

Here Are My Hands

Here are my hands   *(or feet)*
So very small
For you to hang
Upon the wall

And you can watch
As the years go by
How we grow up
My hands and I   *(or feet)*

Another idea for remembering mom or dad on their special days is to have the child write a special card. Have the child decorate the outside. Here are some lines to start out these cards (but the child should dictate most of the card).

- To Mother on her special day (or To Father on his special day)
  This is what I want to say: (write what the child tells you)

- Thank you, Mom, for all you do (or Dad)
  Today it's my turn to help you (include coupons of things child will do)

- Here are some things I'm going to do
  For Mommy because I love you (or Daddy; have child tell you the things to write on their card)

A Favorites Cookbook

Another fun remembrance for mom or dad is a cookbook dictated by the group members. Include their favorite recipes and directions on how you prepare them. This is a wonderful activity to be done over a period of time because it involves the children telling you how to make their favorite foods. This gives children practice in explaining a procedure while using memory and sequencing skills.

The children's ideas on how you cook things, even when you have done cooking activities, is interesting. If you undertake this activity, you will discover that they have an incomplete idea of ingredients, amounts, sequence, and time. Be sure to put each child's name on his recipe. I kept my own son's kindergarten class cookbook and we enjoyed it for years. I gave it back to him and his bride at one of their pre-wedding events, much to the enjoyment of everyone present.

Here is a little verse to accompany your group's collection:

Here are some favorites we like to cook
We tell you how in this little book.
We carefully measured and mixed each dish
And send this to you with a Happy Mother's Day wish. (or Father's Day)

Special Events

A Holiday Is a Special Day

A holiday is a special day
To celebrate with family
In your own special way;
Some families get together
While others go away.

Schools and stores and businesses say:
"Closed for the holiday."
Some holidays are times to play
While some may be a time to pray.
Some holidays are in honor of someone great,
Some are to remember a special date.

There may be parties or picnics or a parade
There may be special foods or decorations made
Some holidays have presents to share,
Or special cards to show you care.

All over the world people celebrate
But their holidays have a different name and date.
No matter how you spend the day
We hope you have a happy holiday.

An Introduction to Holidays

"A Holiday Is a Special Day" introduces most of the key concepts connected with holidays; use this poem to begin talking about holidays. Most young children have a rather fuzzy idea of holidays; they mix them up or think of their birthday as the most important special day. This is normal because they have not been participating in these celebrations long enough to view them with the great sense of tradition that adults attach to them. Children are, however, exposed to the media's presentations and hype on holidays so it is important to approach the subject in appropriate ways in the preschool setting with the emphasis on the concepts suggested by the above poem.

Holidays offer an opportunity to learn about the many different ways families celebrate not only the holidays we know about, but also new ones we can learn about from children and families of different cultural backgrounds. You and your children can also look into holidays celebrated in other countries.

Ask the children to think of a holiday they celebrate and what they did on that holiday. Write down all the holidays they mention and the associations they make. Ask families to tell you about additional holidays they celebrate. Collect as many names and ideas about holidays as you can. You can use this information in many ways.

- Put together books or information sheets about the holidays the children have mentioned and all the ways people celebrate. Ask the librarian for books or information about holidays in other lands to add to your information sheets.

- Use sections from "A Holiday Is a Special Day" as themes for booklets about holidays such as holidays honoring people and holidays for special dates.

- Make holiday murals that include pictures about the holidays in general or of a few particular holidays.

- Use a calendar format to refer to holidays that come up in a particular month and make some plans to acknowledge any holiday of interest to the children with special foods, decorations, a special story or observance, and games or songs.

Use universal themes in thinking about holidays. As you study different celebrations, look for some of the common elements in how holidays are celebrated and focus on those. Some themes occur in many holidays, including customs centered around food, celebrations of light, sharing gifts, attending parades, and dressing in costumes. These also are themes that have appeal to children and lend themselves to child participation activities as some of the following ideas suggest. *The following verses and activities about Hanukkah for example, show how these universal themes apply and how they can be celebrated.* Remember to listen carefully to children and have their curiosity guide you in your planning so as to minimize adult-directed or imposed activities.

◆

A Sample of Winter Celebrations

- Nine Days of Posada (dates vary each year). An extended period of celebration in Mexico reenacting Mary and Joseph's search for shelter (posada means inn); celebrated with parades and pinata parties.

- Kwanzaa (December 26-January 1). An African-American celebration of the traditional African harvest festival (Kwanzaa means first fruits). First observed in the U.S. in 1966, people celebrate Kwanzaa by lighting red, black, or green candles, one for each of the seven days, feasting with family, and discussing the theme for that day. They also exchange small gifts, especially handmade ones stressing the importance of traditional craftsmanship.

- New Year's Eve and Day (December 31 and January 1). The Dutch believe it is good luck to eat something in the shape of a ring on New Year's Eve to represent the circle of the year. In the former Soviet Union, people set up New Year's trees and children attend parties with Granddad Frost and his granddaughter Snow Girl.

- Three Kings Day (January 6; the twelfth day of Christmas). Also called Epiphany. Celebrated with a special surprise cake.

Hanukkah: The Story in Verse

The following verses and activities reflect the celebration of Hanukkah, a Jewish holiday that falls in December. Hanukkah is a festival of light and freedom. It commemorates the victory of a small band of people seeking religious freedom over their Greek rulers. Celebrated by lighting candles (one each for eight nights), family parties, and exchanging of gifts.

On Hanukkah we celebrate
The story of Judah Maccabee
Who fought King Antiochus the great
And won, even with his small army.

He led this special battle, so his people could
Practice their religion, the way they felt they should,
And not have to worship the Greek god Zeus
And the other gods that the king turned loose.

And when they had won this very long fight
They cleaned up the Temple and made it right
They found a little oil to rekindle the Eternal Light
And worried that it wouldn't even last for one night!

But even though the oil was a tiny little bit
For eight days and nights it kept the light lit
Hanukkah is the Hebrew word that means "dedication"
And that is how it came to be a special celebration.

Today on this holiday, when people celebrate
They light special candles numbered one through eight   *(hold up eight fingers)*

This verse provides a rough outline of the story of this holiday; you can find out more from your library. Explain some of the words in this verse that are unfamiliar to the children such as "dedication," "Zeus," and "Eternal Light." If you wish, plan to visit a Jewish synagogue where the children can look at the Jewish symbols in many beautiful forms.

Making Latkes

Although the exact reason is unclear, one of the traditional foods associated with Hanukkah and other family celebrations are latkes (potato pancakes). The following recipe is an easy one to make and the children might enjoy grating and draining the potatoes (if they don't want to prepare the entire two cups, use a food processor, if available). You can buy potato pancake mixes, but they don't provide the same cooking experience. The secret to crispy, delicious potato pancakes is to cook them on a hot, generously greased griddle, which means children must be kept at some distance to avoid spattering hot grease.

Potato Pancakes

2 cups grated, drained potatoes
1/2 cup flour (add to potatoes immediately to keep them white)
2 tablespoons Cream of Wheat cereal
1 teaspoon salt
1/4 teaspoon pepper
1/4 cup water (approximately)
pinch of baking powder

Mix the ingredients together in a large bowl. Drop the mixture by tablespoons onto a hot, generously greased griddle. Fry on both sides. Serve with applesauce and sour cream or syrup.

Counting Candles

Make a Menorah, the special Hanukkah candelabra that holds nine candles, for your flannelboard. Make felt candles and have the children count them (one candle is used to light the others). Say a number and have the children pretend to put up and light that number of candles. Keep changing the number. Make different colored felt candles (red, green, and black are the colors for Kwanzaa; blue and white are Hanukkah colors).

Candle Bright
(Hanukkah or Kwanzaa)

On this night, let us light
One little candle fire   *(hold up one finger)*
This a sight, oh so bright, one little candle fire.

On this night, let us light
Two little candle fires   *(hold up two fingers)*
This a sight, oh so bright, one little candle fire.

  Continue this verse and count to eight for Hanukkah or seven for Kwanzaa, holding up one additional finger for each new number.

Dreidel Song *(traditional)*
(Hanukkah)

I have a little dreidel
I made it out of clay
And when it's dry and ready
Then dreidel I shall play.

Oh, dreidel, dreidel, dreidel
I made it out of clay
Oh, dreidel, dreidel, dreidel
Then dreidel I shall play.

It has a lovely body
With legs so short and thin
And when it is all tired
It drops and then I win.

Oh, dreidel, dreidel, dreidel
With legs so short and thin
Oh, dreidel, dreidel, dreidel
It drops and then I win.

  Instead of buying or making a dreidel, children could pretend to be spinning dreidels and fall on their sides.

Spin the Dreidel

A dreidel is a four-sided top used to play a game that is much like a put and take one. You can buy a dreidel at a synagogue gift shop or make your own with a small box and a pencil (poke the pencil through the center of the box so it will spin). The dreidel has a different Hebrew letter on each side that tells the child what to do. A small group of children play the game using wrapped candies, raisins, tiny marshmallows, or tokens that can be exchanged for treats.

Each child starts with the same number of tokens or treats and puts one in a dish in the center of the circle. Each child takes a turn spinning the top and then takes the action dictated by the letter showing after the top falls over. When the center pot is empty, all children add one item to the pot. The letters and their meanings are:

 Sheen means add a treat to the dish

Hay means the child takes half the treats in the dish

Gimmel means the child takes all the treats in the dish

Nun means the child gets none

In the following examples, the universal themes of presents, food, light and parades are used in general; no reference to a specific holiday is made.

Holidays *(author unknown)*

It's time again for holidays
Hooray, hooray, hooray!   *(clap hands)*
And when I get some brand new toys
I'll play and play and play.   *(imitate actions with toys)*
But there's one thing that I will do
And finish right away.
I'll make a special gift for you   *(pretend to make and wrap gift)*
To wish you a happy day!

Presents

How many presents do I see
Shall we count them, 1, 2, 3
One for Mom, one for Dad, and one for me!   *(hold up a finger on each count)*

4, 5, 6, and even more
Hiding behind the closet door   *(pretend to open door)*
Isn't it fun to look and see
All the pretty presents for our family?

Presenting Presents

- Match the Presents. Wrap a variety of small and medium size boxes in different wrapping papers and let children sort them into shoe boxes, which you wrapped in matching paper. Variation: Wrap tops and bottoms of boxes separately and let children find the matching sets.

- Dramatic Play. Set up a gift shop with cash register, play money, shopping bags, and gifts from school or home (books, toys, kitchen items, hats, mittens, odds and ends). Provide gift boxes, newspaper or tissue, and tape for wrapping. Children can make varieties of printed paper to use as gift wrap in the gift shop.

- Guessing Game. Have one child dramatize a present they would like to get (or did get) and let the others guess what it is.

A Tasting Verse

Pretzels are salty, oranges are sweet
Lemons are sour, ice cream is a treat
Crackers are crunchy, popcorn is munchy
Apples are chewy, caramel is gooey
At holiday times, there's lots to eat
Tasting new things is really neat!

Take a Little Apple
(to the tune of "I'm a Little Teapot")

Take a little apple, cut it up   *(imitate all actions)*
Put it in a pot and cook it up
When it gets all mushy, mash it up
Now it's applesauce let's eat it up

Do I Like It?

Talk about the taste and textures of foods.

- Sweet and sour. Use oranges and lemons to contrast the taste. Squeeze some lemons and pour the juice into a pitcher of water. Let the children taste the unsweetened (sour) lemonade. Add sugar and then taste again. Squeeze some oranges and pour the juice into another pitcher of water. Let the children taste the orange juice. Compare its taste to the lemon juice.
- Crunchy and soft. Compare foods that are crunchy (such as crackers, pretzels, apples, and raw vegetables) to soft ones (such as pudding, ice cream, and applesauce).
- Salty and unsalty. Make popcorn and sample with and without salt. Compare snacks such as dried fruit and raisins with trail mix snacks.

Sort foods such as nuts, fruits, and vegetables into categories by type of food. Include subcategories such as citrus fruits. Notice likenesses and difference in types of foods when assigning them to categories. Bring in samples of foods in different forms and discuss how the food is treated to get to the particular form. Some samples are: apples, applesauce, and dried apples (bring in different colored apples and taste them to see if color makes a difference); peanuts and peanut butter; oranges and orange juice (and other food and juice combinations); grapes and raisins; potatoes and potato chips. Try making some of these items. Write about your results and discuss them.

I'm a Little Candle
(to the tune of "I'm a Little Teapot")

I'm a little candle, shining bright
Here is my flame that gives the light   *(place two hands together above head)*

When I get all burned up, you will see.
There will be nothing left of me   *(children slowly go down and curl up on floor)*

Oh, Do You See
(to the tune of "The Muffin Man")

Oh, do you see the candle's glow
The candle's glow, the candle's glow?
Oh, do you see the candle's glow
It's such a pretty sight!

Candle Counting Chant

One little, two little, three little candles

(hold up one finger as you say each number)

Four little, five little, six little candles
Seven little, eight little, nine little candles
Ten little candle lights

(repeat, counting backwards. Lower fingers as you count backwards)

Candle Lights

Make paper candles and candle holders. Use toilet paper tubes for the candles. Cover them with colorful wrapping paper or foil. Stuff them with red, yellow, or orange tissue paper allowing a little paper to stick up from the tube to form the flame. Place the tube candles on an inverted egg carton, which can serve as the candle holder. If you wish, decorate the egg carton sides with paint or glitter. Use the candles as you sing "I'm a Little Candle," "Oh, Do You See," and "Candle Counting Chant." You can also cut the egg cartons into smaller sections to make smaller candle holders. Use them as table decorations.

Demonstrate lighting a candle, observe its flame. Gently blow on the flame or move the candle slowly and observe how the flame moves or flickers. Have children imitate the flame's movements with their fingers, arms, or whole bodies. Let the children pretend to be candles; one child lights the candles and they all flicker and burn slowly down. A wind could also blow them out and the process is repeated.

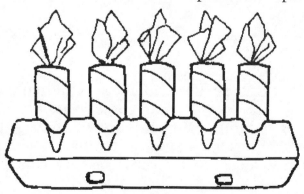

Here Comes the Parade
(to the tune of "I am a Great Musician")

See here comes the big parade
Marching down the street   *(clap hands as you chant)*
Who will join the big parade
Marching down the street?

We will, Oh, we will   *(children march and form a parade)*
The little children said
We will join the big parade
Marching down the street.

See here comes the big parade
Marching down the street   *(clap hands as you march)*
Everyone must keep the beat   *(clap and march to beat)*
Marching down the street   *(repeat as often as needed for a parade)*

We will, Oh we will
The little children said
We will keep the beat
Marching down the street.   *(Repeat song as often as needed for the parade.)*

Flags

Flags are flying in the breeze
Stars and stripes in colors that please
In the U.S.A. it's red, white, and blue
In other countries, it's a different hue
We all love our flag and raise it high
And celebrate with parades marching by.

Here We Come!

   Talk about the holidays that have parades and ask the children if they have been to a
parade. Let them tell you what they know about parades and the things in them.
Organize some parades using rhythm instruments and small flags. Talk about flags in
other countries (the United Nations has a huge selection) and when other countries
might have parades. Some parades are part of community celebrations and are not really

holidays—but a parade is a parade! Pay attention to local festivals and explain how they are different from national holidays. Local festivals are often of more immediate interest in the community and should be treated much the same way as holidays as far as sharing in their celebration with the children.

Boom, Boom, Boom

Boom, boom, boom
Hear the stirring drum.   *(beat imaginary drums)*
Boom, boom, boom
See the marchers come.   *(march around)*
Flags are waving   *(wave imaginary flags)*
Trumpets braying   *(play imaginary trumpets)*
Boom, boom, boom
Now the marching's done.

See the Floats

See the floats all in a row
Lined up to parade and ready to go.
The first one is all dressed in lace
The second one has a funny face.
The third one is covered with flowers and fruit
The fourth one has a horn to toot.
The drums begin, the trumpets blow
Watch the floats as off they go.

You could recite this verse with a parade of floats made by the children.

Props for Parades

- Make floats out of shoe box lids. Decorate with tissue or crepe paper. Set up a display of floats or attach them with string to small cars. Let the children push the cars with floats attached to form a parade.

- Make larger floats using the tops of larger boxes such as department store gift boxes. Use pipe cleaner figures and odds and ends from home or school (such as doll house furniture, cartoon figures, and small animal figures) to decorate the floats. Make room in larger floats for dolls or stuffed animals. Let the children plan and decorate the floats and decide what things they need to complete them. Use Tinkertoy building blocks and wheels for moving bases for small floats. Giant Tinkertoy building blocks or trucks can move the bigger floats.

- Make military hats for your parades. Cut a plastic jug 5-1/2 inches from the bottom. Use the upper portion of the jug to form the major part of the hat. Cut a visor shape piece of cardboard, leaving small points or tabs at each end. Staple tabs inside plastic jug. Attach a piece of construction paper above the visor. Make a plume by cutting strips of construction paper. Attach to straw or strips of thin cardboard and insert into the pour spout of the jug.

Watching

I looked out of the skyway
And what did I see
Cars whizzing by underneath me
The people beneath me looked rather small
And I saw the tops of heavy trucks and all
I like to look down from way up on top
And not have to wait for the traffic to stop.

A skyway is a great place to be
When a parade is passing by
It really is so easy to see
When your window is up so high
I see the marchers lift their knees
As the musicians start to play
And parts of the floats that no one sees
As they start to roll this way

Wonder what a float would look like from up above?
What would I see that no one else does?

Special Places

Under the Circus Tent

What wondrous things you're sure to see
If you enter the circus tent with me   *(walk in circle)*
Three big rings on the circus floor   *(hold up three fingers)*
With animals, acrobats, clowns, and more

As the fancy horses begin to prance   *(prance in place)*
The dressed up dogs do a little dance   *(children dance)*
The drums and trumpets are loudly playing   *(imitate playing)*
"Watch ring number one," an announcer is saying.   *(cup hands over mouth)*

Some people are balancing on a high wire   *(pretend to balance)*
Sliding and riding on top of a little tire
Under the circus tent is an amazing place
But if I get scared, I cover my face.   *(cover face with hands)*

Let's Pretend Circus

Ask the children if they have been to a circus and discuss the things they liked or didn't like there. Did any of them feel scared at the circus? What things made them feel that way? What things made them laugh? Ask them if they have seen any parades connected to a circus. What things were different about a circus parade?

It is fun to plan a circus parade with children. Let them decide what to have in their parade and if they would like to act out some circus acts. Usually children love acting out parades with marching, wearing special hats or dress clothes, and imitating various animals or other circus acts. Let them collect their own props and items for their parade and plan when and where to hold it. Provide a box or place for them to keep all their circus paraphernalia so that they can hold as many parades or pretend circuses as they like. Allow them to start simple and get more elaborate as they continue or expand their circus play.

The Circus

We went to the circus and what did we see?
Clowns doing tricks as silly as could be   *(do floppy clown acts)*
Lions and monkeys jumping through hoops   *(jump through pretend hoops)*
Trapeze artists doing loop de loops   *(pretend to fly through air)*
We went to the circus and what did we do?
We ate cotton candy and hot dogs, too.   *(pretend to eat)*

Discuss the special vocabulary words used in these circus verses. Collect pictures that illustrate these words and discuss them with the children. Put them in a Circus World shoe box to use for continuing discussion.

◆

Clowns

Clowns are marching in the circus parade   *(pretend to march)*
They wear the funniest clothes ever made,
Watch those floppy, floppy clowns   *(let bodies do floppy things)*
They make funny faces
From smiles to frowns   *(make funny faces)*
They do a lot of silly tricks   *(do tricks)*
Some are even doing flips   *(bend up and down)*
They seem to have lots of ups and downs.   *(jump and fall down)*

Elephants *(traditional)*

The elephant has a great big trunk   *(extend arms with palms touching each other)*

That goes swinging to and fro   *(swing from side to side)*
And he has tiny, tiny eyes   *(form tiny slits with index fingers and thumbs)*

That show him where to go
His huge big ears go flopping   *(wear elephant ears headdresses or cup hands near ears)*

Flopping up and down   *(move head up and down)*
And his great big feet go stomping
Stomping on the ground   *(stomp heavily as you march bent over; swing arms and move heads so ears flop)*

Elephant Ears

Make elephant ears for each child to wear in a circus parade. For each set, you will need two sheets of gray construction paper, a gray headband (you can make your own headband out of strips of gray paper about 2 inches wide), a large rubber band, stapler, and scissors.

Staple a rubber band to each end of the headband for adjustable and easy-to-wear bands. For each ear, round off the edges of three sides of the gray paper (leave the upper inside corner uncut). Fold the uncut corner in about 12 inches from the edge. Staple the folded edge to the side of the headband so that the rest of the sheet hangs down and the fold faces the back.

I'm a Great Big Lion *(traditional)*

I'm a great big lion	
You can hear me roar!	*(roar)*
I've had my dinner but I	
Want some more!	*(pretend to eat)*

Leo Lion *(traditional)*

I'm a little bit afraid when I hear	
Leo Lion roar!	*(children roar)*
But I like him when he's sleeping	
'Cuz he doesn't even snore!	*(lay lion puppet or hand down to sleep)*

The Lion

The lion is a ferocious beast	*(act fierce and roar like a lion)*
His roaring makes me hide	*(hide behind hands)*
I'm glad he's locked up in a cage	*(pretend to lock up cage like a lion tamer)*
And we are all outside!	*(fold arms and smile)*

Paper Plate Lions

Paint the outer rim of a paper plate yellowish brown. Let the children fringe around the plate. Draw lion faces in the middle of the plate or glue on features. Attach the paper plate lions to tongue blades for lion puppets. Use with the lion verses. Have some children be lions in the circus parade.

The Amusement Park

Amusement parks are noisy places	*(cover ears)*
With rides zooming all around,	*(zoom hand up and down)*
The people on them start screaming	*(make silent screams)*
When the ride plunges down toward the ground	*(make hand plunge down)*

I used to be afraid when I was two
But now there are lots of things I like to do

I like to go on a little train	
That rides all over the park	*(pretend to drive train)*
It goes into a tunnel—	*(say "toot, toot")*
And we all scream in the dark!	*(cup hands over mouth and pretend to scream)*

I like to fly the airplanes	
Way above the ground	*(pretend to fly)*
And ride in the boats and the cars	
Around and around	*(pretend to drive)*

I go jump up and down in the bubble	*(jump up and down)*
And ride on the merry-go-round.	
At the park, to stay out of trouble,	
Stay close together and no running around.	

Amusement Park Mural

Talk with the children about any of their experiences at amusement parks. Let them tell you about any special types of theme or local amusement parks that they have been to. What do they like to do at the park?

Make a mural by writing the things the children tell you across the top and then have them illustrate their words. Magazines and brochures may have pictures to add to the children's drawings. Make a list of safety rules for such parks. Remind the children about the importance of safety rules in these places.

The Pizza Parlor

There's a pizza parlor that's a special place
It has a large costumed character with a funny face
He walks around and waves "hello"
And tells you to watch his special show.

They play music and sing songs too
And always sing "Happy Birthday to You."
They have games galore,
Great climbing places and more!
This too is a rather noisy place
'Cuz children are playing in all its space.

Can the children guess the name of this special place from the above verse? Let them tell you about their experiences with similar restaurants that have playgrounds and entertainment. Have they been to parties there? Write up something about what happened at the parties, what they did, and what was the most fun. What didn't they like in either of these settings?

Where Is It?

A place we go quite frequently
That is a favorite for my friends and me
Has hamburgers to eat and a whole lot more
And a special playground right next door.

There are tunnels and slides that look quite neat
And a place to jump in balls that cover your feet
Lots of things for children to play
I wish we could go there every day.

Ask the children if they can guess the place this poem describes. There may be several different answers of places that fit this description from fast food restaurants to kids' gyms. Write down the places the children suggest and ask them what they like to do or eat at the sites they mention. Compile all the children's answers into a booklet on children's eating and playing ventures. Include all their comments on their favorite foods and any observations about the special features of each place such as special deals, gifts or souvenirs, and birthday party features.

The Playground

There's another kind of playground
Where I like to go
With swings, slides, and climbers, high and low,
And something you push to make it go round
And teeter-totters that can go up and down
There's a house like a fort and a sandbox, too
And fancy climbing spaces that are red, yellow, and blue
There are some bouncy horses to ride
But my favorite is the curving slide.

The World's Greatest Playground

   Make up a large poster of the greatest playground. Let the children list all the things they think should be in a great playground. Let them look through equipment and store catalogs to pick out items. Do they come up with any unusual ideas like an old boat, car, or fanciful items like a Batmobile? Let them illustrate their playground with drawings or picture cutouts.

◆

A Birthday Party

I went to a birthday party
That was really kind of neat
A magician did some tricks
We had cake and ice cream to eat.

The only thing I think that was kind of a bore
Was when they opened all the presents, while we sat on the floor
I wish I had gotten to open presents, too
But that's not what they usually do.

Maybe on my birthday, I'll start something new
And let other kids open presents, too!
Of course, all the presents would still be for me.
But it might be more fun to let other kids see.

All about Birthday Parties

Birthday parties are, of course, the major special event in most young children's lives. From about age three, when they first seem to become aware of the significance of this event, birthday parties take on great importance in each child's life—his or her own party that is! Other children's parties are not nearly as important except when one four-year-old angrily tells another that she won't invite her to her birthday party because of some momentary offense.

"A Birthday Party" brings up the topic of going to other people's parties, which probably has many ups and downs as the verse implies. This is a good way to discuss how it feels to give others presents and wait while those presents are opened. Write down the things children tell you about these events such as favorite places for birthday parties, what they like best, things they don't like, and a time they got upset.

Birthday parties are sometimes stressful for children because of all the excitement, the unfamiliar environments, the number of children present, possible noise level, not to mention the stress the adults involved may feel. It is a good idea to discuss things that can sometimes be upsetting and how to help others who might be upset. Keep your lists to take out and read again when the children are talking about a birthday party. See if there are new items to add to those lists.

Our Children's Museum

Our children's museum is the most fun
It has something special for everyone
You can try what it's like to be on TV
Or look at some creatures that live in the sea

There's a grocery store that is just my size
And a place to dress up in a fancy disguise.
There's a hospital corner with real things to explore
And a bus and a train and a whole lot more.
It's great to go to this special place
And see all the smiles on everyone's face.

   Did children's museums get mentioned on the birthday party lists you compiled?
Those lists might be good to share with parents who may be looking for ideas for future
parties. In visiting museums, be sure to establish safety procedures and rules for keeping
the group together.

A State Fair

Sometimes we go to a great big fair
I think everyone in the world is there
We park our car miles away
And it seems like we're walking all the day.

There's a lot to see and a lot to do
Animals, rides, and exhibits, too
There are all sorts of things on display
And a midway with all kinds of games to play.

In the grandstand, there's a great big show
With fireworks afterwards, you know!
I get lots of fun things to eat
But fairs sure are hard on your feet!

Places We Go

Write up some stories about the places children in your group have been and save them as the year progresses. When you have collected several of these, put them together into a book titled "Special Places" or some other name the group picks. Read the book with the group from time to time and continue writing new stories for your second volume.

Other Redleaf Press Publications

Basic Guide to Family Child Care Record Keeping : Fourth Edition— Clear instructions on keeping necessary family day care business records.

Calendar-Keeper — Activities, family day care record keeping, recipes and more. Updated annually. Most popular publication in the field.

Child Care Resource & Referral Counselors & Trainers Manual — Both a ready reference for the busy phone counselor and a training guide for resource and referral agencies.

Developing Roots & Wings: A Trainer's Guide to Affirming Culture In Early Childhood Programs — The training guide for Root & Wings, with 11 complete sessions and over 170 training activities.

The Dynamic Infant — Combines an overview of child development with innovative movement and sensory experiences for infants and toddlers.

Early Childhood Super Director — The first book of management strategies specifically for the early childhood director.

Family Child Care Contracts and Policies — Samples contracts and policies, and how - to information on using them effectively to improve tour business.

Family Child Care Tax Workbook — Updated every year, latest step-by-step information on forms, depreciation, etc.

Heart to Heart Caregiving: A Sourcebook of Family Day Care Activities, Projects and Practical Provider Support — Excellent ideas and guidance written by an experienced provider.

Kids Encyclopedia of Things to Make and Do — Nearly 2,000 art and craft projects for children aged 4-10.

The (No Leftovers!) Child Care Cookbook — Over 80 child-tested recipes and 20 menus suitable for family child care providers and center programs. CACFP creditable.

Open the Door, Let's Explore — Full of fun, inexpensive neighborhood walks and field trips designed to help young children.

Pathways to Play — Help children improve their play skills with a skill checklist and planned activities.

Practical Solutions to Practically Every Problem: The Early Childhood Teacher's Manual — Over 300 proven developmentally appropriate solutions for all kinds of classroom problems.

Roots & Wings: Affirming Culture in Early Childhood Programs — A new approach to multicultural education that helps shape positive attitudes toward cultural differences.

Staff Orientation in Early Childhood Programs — Complete manual for orienting new staff on all program areas.

Teachables From Trashables — Step-by-step guide to making over 50 fun toys from recycled household junk.

Teachables II — Similar to *Teachables From Trashables*; with another 75-plus toys.

Those Mean Nasty Dirty Downright Disgusting but... Invisible Germs — A delightful story that reinforces for children the benefits of frequent hand washing.

Trusting Toddlers: Planning for One to Three Year Olds in Child Care Centers — Expert panel explains how to set up toddler programs that really work

CALL FOR CATALOG OR ORDERING INFORMATION 1-800-423-8309